The Art of
Captivating
Conversation

The Art of
Captivating
Conversation

How to be
Confident
Charismatic
Likable
in any situation

PATRICK KING

Skyhorse Publishing

Skyhorse Publishing books may be purchased in bulk at special discounts for sales promotion, corporate gifts, fund-raising, or educational purposes. Special editions can also be created to specifications. For details, contact the Special Sales Department, Skyhorse Publishing, 307 West 36th Street, 11th Floor, New York, NY 10018 or info@skyhorsepublishing.com.

Skyhorse® and Skyhorse Publishing® are registered trademarks of Skyhorse Publishing, Inc.®, a Delaware corporation.

Visit our website at www.skyhorsepublishing.com.

10 9 8 7 6 5 4

Library of Congress Cataloging-in-Publication Data is available on file.

Cover design by Daniel Brount

Print ISBN: 978-1-5107-2906-3
Ebook ISBN: 978-1-5107-2907-0

Printed in China

Table of Contents

Introduction

It's probably fair to say that I have a lot of titles at this point: social skills and conversation coach, social interaction specialist, international best-selling author, teacher, consultant, course designer, former dating coach, former corporate lawyer—the list goes on.

But in the grand scheme of things, none of those titles really matter, and they certainly aren't what might qualify me to write this book. The only title that matters in that regard is that I was a late bloomer.

What exactly does that have to do with *The Art of Captivating Conversation?* I think it's important to hear these words coming from a former self-proclaimed social recluse who used to have trouble answering the telephone, because it means that these types of dynamic skills that will get you far in life absolutely not are innate; they are learnable with some elbow grease and sweat.

When I was a young man, I was massively shy and anxious around others. I had managed to convince myself that I was in the top .01 percent of introverts, but in hindsight, it's clear that was just an excuse for me to shrink into my shell and avoid social situations. When I would go to a restaurant, I would be sweaty when the waiter or waitress came to me to ask for my order. I would rehearse my order endlessly inside my head so I could squeeze out "A double cheeseburger and a diet coke" flawlessly.

Mail would pile up in my mailbox constantly because every time I wanted to retrieve it, either the mailman or a neighbor would be there and I didn't want to interact with them.

Cheery cashiers at the grocery store were my nightmare, and I would always pick the line with the cashier who seemed the quietest.

God forbid I was required to attend a networking event where I was in a room full of virtual strangers. I'd rather swallow broken glass.

I didn't realize it at the time, but I was allowing my life to be ruled by fear—fear of judgment, rejection, and failure. I looked at the people in the center of the room with a sense of envy and amazement while feeling that I just wasn't meant for that type of social life.

I carried on like this for much of my adolescence until a pivotal moment my third year of college where I was spending something like my sixth Friday night in a row alone at home. I lived with three roommates but rarely saw them because they were always out enjoying what I thought were activities that just weren't for people like me. I glanced through my planner, blank and devoid of social obligations. I suddenly decided to act upon it and change the type of person I was right then and there.

I had reached what I would later call my critical mass of discontent—this sense of discontent with my social life was far stronger than any fear that was holding me back.

The following three months were marked by constant anxiety as I slowly pushed the boundaries of my comfort zone. I had to build my sense of social confidence brick by brick and constantly remind myself that I wasn't only as confident as my most recent foray. I adopted a policy of never saying "no," and always saying "yes." I began to flex social muscles that had been dormant since I was a child with no concept of judgment. By the end of the school year, I was regularly spending time with my roommates who admitted that they would previously avoid me in the house if I was in common areas because I was so socially stunted.

This is the point in my life I refer to when I say that I bloomed, and that's why my self-imposed title of late bloomer is so important.

It's not helpful for a chronic introvert to hear advice from someone who has always been that person in the center of the room. They may be successful, but they won't be able to deconstruct and explain their actions because it's been so instinctual and natural to them. It's the advice equivalent of someone who grew to be seven feet tall at age thirteen telling people that it's simple to be a basketball player—you just need to grow taller.

While that's true, it's not information that people can use and incorporate into their daily lives. Useful information in the course of teaching comes from those who understand struggle and pain, and ultimately share the process used to relieve themselves of that pain. You already understand *why* you picked this book up. You're reading this book for the *how*, and that's what I hope to arm you with in spades. You've seen where I came from; obviously something worked.

How did I end up coaching and teaching social and conversation skills? That's another story in itself.

I used to be a corporate lawyer, but it quickly became apparent that I absolutely hated every aspect of it—not uncommon by itself. I also found that it was a terrible fit for my personality. Things I had prided myself on, such as my interpersonal skills, personality, and sense of creativity, were traits that were expressly rejected by the law.

Law, in fact, is about jamming everything in your path into the strict confines dictated by thousands of cases over the years, which means that your role is essentially a high-priced hammer. That's why lawyers are seen as risk-averse—they're just acting within those strict confines. After I graduated and began to work full-time, I can safely say that I started to dread going into work by the third week. Like someone who had married a partner who turned out to be lying about their identity, I developed a wandering eye.

I always had a keen interest in human interaction and dating—it was what I would always talk about in my free time, with friends and even strangers. I just liked hearing about these situations and dissecting them to understand the *why*. "Tell me about your date" and "what did he text you afterwards" were always more compelling to me than asking about someone's work.

Introduction

On a lark, I started offering to write online dating profiles for my friends so I could hear more of these stories. When you do anything that many times, you develop a systemized approach, and on another lark, I decided to publish my first book on online dating.

The book sold unexpectedly well, so I started coaching, and I also became a matchmaker, working for some of Silicon Valley's richest for a short period of time.

What was ultimately missing, however, was that it felt like I was only teaching principles that were designed to lead to a very limited set of outcomes—getting or seducing someone. In the grand scheme of things, it started to feel insignificant, and even though a younger me would have loved that knowledge, a younger me would have been in dire need of more foundational, holistic skills.

Conversation and social skills are about as basic and foundational as you can get—they are the building blocks of all relationships, romantic or not. They are the tools we use every day without realizing it, and they are the gatekeepers we must pass through to begin a friendship.

So why not sharpen those skills to make an impact on everyone you meet, not just someone you want to charm and seduce?

Everyone has heard the maxim that it's not what you know, but who you know that moves you forward in life. I would contend that it's an incomplete saying. It's not only who you know, but it's who likes you that gets you ahead in life.

Even when I was a lawyer counting the hours until lunch, I was still able to get any job I wanted, despite my average grades, because of my interpersonal skills and ability to connect with others. In the workplace, skills can generally be learned, but "fit" and chemistry cannot. It's the same with your friends—you don't necessarily care about what they can do, you just care that you make each other laugh and understand one another.

These realizations led me to nickname my overall philosophy towards conversation and social skills as "the greasy crowbars" of life.

Who uses greasy crowbars? You got it: burglars and general reprobates. Despite that, it's definitely a good thing.

Conversation and social skills are greasy crowbars because they give you access to new people and places. After all, who determines the arbitrary boundaries that objectively separate people? They give you opportunities and chances to go beyond where you otherwise would. They open doors you would never have been able to open by yourself, and once they're open, you can prove that you are indeed worthy.

Let's say you're interviewing for a job that might be slightly out of reach. However, you happen to hit it off with the interviewers and they like you. To the interviewer and the company, is it more important to work with people they like who can eventually learn the skills, or someone who knows the skills but that they don't like? It's not even close.

The greasy crowbar philosophy sums up why conversation skills are so important. You never know when a single conversation can dramatically change your life, and if you start looking at conversation like a window ready to be pried open, then you'll give yourself considerably more opportunities in anything you want to achieve—socially or professionally.

You can lever yourself into the position you might not be 100 percent qualified for, or as my client Michael discovered, you can use conversation as the greasy crowbar to a more unified and peaceful workplace dynamic. Or as another client, Rob, discovered, you can win over your hostile mother-in-law who was destined to hate you because you moved her daughter to the other side of the country.

When you can start to master conversation skills, foundational towards everything you'd want in life, you can start to make the distinct shift to viewing social situations as opportunities instead of chances to bomb and feel bad about yourself. A room full of people is suddenly turned into a bunch of friendly faces and new friends versus people who are living to judge you and rip you apart.

With that said, *The Art of Captivating Conversation* has two distinct goals. First, I want to solve the problem of living life through fear and anxiety like I once did and provide the confidence and mindset to be the engaging person you've always been jealous of. Second, I want to give you the actual tools to charm people's socks off and leave them chasing after you. Get to the party, and then know what to do once you're there.

Sounds just like what the late bloomer in me could use!

Chapter 1
The Patterns We Live

When most people are hesitant about improving their conversation or social skills, it's because we feel like conversations are a black hole. No light gets in and no light gets out. You have no idea what's going on inside, and if you get too close, you will get sucked in and never escape with your self-esteem intact.

Conversations seem like an unpredictable mystery.

Who knows what is going to happen? What topics will come up? How can you even prepare for something that inherently has no structure and has no defined end point? And when you get thrown into a topic or line of thought you didn't see coming, you are destined to commit a social atrocity of such magnitude that the ensuing awkward silence will turn people off of you for the foreseeable future.

Something like that, anyway.

Point being, it's easy to see conversation and social interaction as inherently unpredictable because they involve other human beings. We aren't dealing with actors armed with scripts—we are dealing with people, and these people have the ability to swing into any direction you can imagine. You might innocently think you are just mentioning the weather or the traffic, and all of a sudden they start reminiscing about their recently deceased dog. You freeze and desperately scramble for what to do now. You weren't prepared for this.

Now, you have to wing it and think on your feet, and this can be a particularly frightening prospect for many people. Topics of social conversations can run the gamut and when it feels so open-ended, you can't help but visualize the worst-case scenario of saying something awkward, someone deeming you to be stupid, and then becoming a social pariah overnight.

However, think for a second about how you might approach a job interview. You'd still be nervous about it, but markedly less so because there is a clear purpose. You know what will come up, your main talking points, and probably what the interviewer will bring up.

This knowledge lets you know exactly what to prepare for in a very clear way, and it's not surprising that job interviews, while nerve wracking for completely different reasons, can be less stressful than a birthday party.

Because the purpose is to investigate if you are a good fit for the job, you know the anecdotes and comments that will portray that. The main talking points will be related to the company, your qualifications and fit, how you might perform in hypothetical situations, and the interviewer will ask about stories to showcase these traits you supposedly possess.

You know there's a certain structure and procedure your interviewer will follow. You probably even know the first five questions you will be asked, and the general range of topics you may cover. What's more, you even know how to answer these questions and topics in a way that reflects you the best and which pushes the conversation forward.

Now, you might think that the ability to prepare for conversations and social interactions is strictly related to artificial settings, such as a job interview, where there is a clear purpose.

Here's a proposal that will fundamentally change how you view conversation: conversations can be extremely predictable because there actually is a clear purpose to most of them, and people are looking for a very small subset of things. For this reason, they are predictable, and they can be as easy to navigate as a job interview.

Purpose and main interest → preparation → less anxiety
→ smooth conversation

For a job interview, you know what the deal is. So what's the deal for social conversations? What is the purpose and main interest?

The Primary Purposes of Conversation

Though it seems like conversation comes in all shapes and forms, we actually engage in social conversation for very few reasons.

Similarly, while we might feel like we are expressing and feeling the rainbow of emotions, there are in actuality only six primary emotions: happiness, sadness, fear, anger, surprise, and disgust. A recent study even proposed that there are only four main emotions, lumping fear and surprise, and anger and disgust, together.[*]

If we meet an old friend and are eagerly telling them about our recent date, or recounting a story about being cut off in traffic, or asking them about their latest vacation—it may seem like there are different purposes for these stories, but they actually all come together in one—entertainment and pleasure.

For the purposes of simplicity, I like to boil conversation down to two general purposes:

1. Entertainment and pleasure
2. Utility

Just about every reason you have to engage with others will fall into these two categories. Just like with the rainbow of emotions you think you might be expressing, they are usually just variations of the six primary emotions. Just about every joke, story, assertion, or comment you make falls into one of these two purposes.

Entertainment and pleasure is the simple act of making yourself happier. We feel validated and connected when we are able to share our emotions with others and solicit their feedback. When we tell people about our troubles, we are seeking sympathy and solutions, and ultimately to feel better about ourselves. A positive story about climbing a mountain

---

* Jack, R. E., Sun, W., Delis, I., Garrod, O. G. B. and Schyns, P. G. (2016) Four not six: revealing culturally common facial expressions of emotion. Journal of Experimental Psychology: General, 145(6), pp. 708–730.

provides pleasure from approval, while a negative story about a car crash provides pleasure from social support.

We are driven to connect deeply with others because it gives us pleasure and keeps us preoccupied.

Seeking to crack a joke or make a funny observation about the wallpaper? You want to share your sense of amusement with others and bask in the validation their laughter gives you.

Entertainment and pleasure is the single biggest goal people are seeking when they engage with others, and sometimes we forget about this when we get caught up in small talk. Humans are innately pleasure-seeking and pain-avoiding, which is where social support comes in. Make no mistake about it—entertainment and pleasure is the biggest purpose to conversation that we constantly forget about.

People talk to others who entertain them and make them feel good. That's really as simple as it can get, and it's no more complex than that. If you can satisfy this purpose, people will like you, want to be friends with you, and seek out your company. Thankfully, there are actually many ways to accomplish this goal.

The second primary purpose people engage with others is to accomplish something.

We interact with others to increase our utility and usefulness. If you are asking questions about how long an interview will run, you are doing so because it will allow you to prepare better for it. If you are telling a story about your weekend, it might only be to provide context so you can help someone else plan their own weekend. It may also give us pleasure, but the overall reason is to achieve something directly or indirectly.

The purpose of interaction here is transactional; for example, speaking to a cashier while you buy your groceries, giving instructions to people, or asking for directions to the closest Starbucks. We aren't seeking pleasure directly in these situations, though it may be attached to accomplishing something. This is probably true of the minority of social conversations, and is often combined with the first purpose of entertainment and pleasure.

Understanding the main purposes of an interaction gets us a little bit closer to that feeling of predictability we have going into a job interview. But there are additional ways we can make social conversations more predictable so we can conduct ourselves in a manner that makes them flow better and more smoothly.

Hello, Gorg

We only have to look to human nature to be able to consistently predict where an interaction will go. In fact, we can look at a primitive man called Gorg from the year 10,000 BC to see how he still colors our interactions to this day.

Gorg is selfish and self-interested. This isn't necessarily a negative trait. It's just that no one else cares about Gorg and his interests the way he does, so he inherently must prioritize himself above everything else. His life is spent looking out for his own survival amongst saber-toothed tigers and poisonous plants. Everyone else is busy doing the same, so it's by necessity that he is selfish and self-interested. He'd rather he himself eat and survive than have a friend eat and survive. That's how it works in his world.

He spends his time thinking about *his* problems, *his* triumphs, and *his* well-being. In the past, he has occasionally put others before himself, but ended up having his arm nearly bitten off. It was a difficult lesson he learned. Nowadays, he concerns himself only with his cave, his food stores, and his collection of spears.

Gorg sometimes looks into a still pond and sees only himself (though he isn't sure what he's looking at). He spends his time alone and in isolation. He feels that there is a wealth of thoughts battling inside his head that are valuable and important, but he has no one to share them with.

When Gorg does interact with other primitive folk, he is typically working together with them to find food or shelter. What's more, he knows he must prove himself to be valuable among the others so he can continue to be sought out and included in their survival efforts. He showcases his talents and strength while killing boar and makes sure he receives recognition and social validation from the others. One year he couldn't hunt effectively because he was hurt, so he still found a way to support the others where he could. If he doesn't fit in, so to speak, he may become an outcast and be left to starve during the harsher months of the year. He knows the utmost importance of not being socially rejected by the group at large.

Gorg never does more work than he needs to. He enjoys a lazy day spent painting his cave, but it's more because he must conserve energy for the unpredictable parts of his life. He is accustomed to putting in the minimum amount of effort he needs so he can be ready for an unexpected five-mile hunt of a deer, or be able to take six hours to find enough firewood to keep warm at night. He never does anything just for the sake of doing it unless he sees a clear purpose, or a clear benefit, such as allowing himself to be lazier in the future. This sense of laziness also affects his habits in how he interacts with other people. He has become accustomed to a certain way of doing things and isn't interested in putting in the effort to change them.

It ain't broke, so it ain't getting fixed, says Gorg.

Finally, Gorg almost drowned once when he was trying to catch a fish. He didn't enjoy that. Now he avoids the water whenever possible, minus his monthly bath in which he only braves water that goes up to his stomach.

Gorg has a tough life—the moment he steps outside his cave, he doesn't know if he's going to be mauled to death by a rampaging bear. Twelve thousand years later, we really aren't very different from primitive Gorg.

In fact, we are driven by the exact same facets of human nature that drive Gorg.

The subject of "me" occupies the vast majority of our thoughts and makes us inherently selfish. We seek validation and approval from others for our social confidence and survival. We are by nature lazy and seek to expend as little effort as possible, and are also driven by bad habits that become cemented over time. We seek pleasure and avoid pain.

When we combine the two primary purposes of social conversation with what we know about basic human nature, we can begin to see clear patterns and predictability in how we interact with others.

Specifically, this leads to three patterns in conversation, which make it, as you might have guessed, fairly predictable and job interview–like.

Conversation Patterns

Conversation Pattern #1: People just want to be entertained and receive pleasure from a conversation

This is subjective, and it may take indirect forms, but people enjoy speaking to other people who engage, interest, fascinate, shock, and otherwise entertain them. This is why most people tend to hate small talk—it is the opposite of entertaining and pleasurable. It is usually on a small set of topics that no one cares about, and it is clear that both parties are just going through the motion and ritual of uttering platitudes.

> *Looks like it might rain.*
> *Yup, good thing I brought my umbrella today!*

For instance, when people go to see a movie, they feel that a movie is going to be entertaining and give them pleasure. That's all that matters in the grand scheme of things. Of course, the type of movie matters, but the overall goal is entertainment and that drastically defines how the movie is chosen.

And so it should drastically define your approach to conversations. People are interested in being interested. If you're not getting pleasure from a conversation, is the only thing keeping you in that conversation a desire to avoid being socially awkward?

Your topics, responses, stories, and questions—do they accomplish that goal? What is *the other person* getting out of it, not you? We find that our mindset changes drastically when we resist our instinctual selfishness and think about how others will benefit. In other words, how can we act in conversation to allow them to be selfish?

Thankfully, there are many ways to accomplish this goal that we will go over throughout this book.

Conversation Pattern #2: People want validation and to feel like they matter

We aren't necessarily seeking parental approval and a pat on the back, but we are seeking positive feedback from others because with that comes the avoidance of rejection and judgment.

Whatever we share and discuss, we are seeking understanding, belonging, relatability, and empathy. Above all else, we are seeking an accepting smile of understanding, and the sense that people understand our emotions.

Without these valuable tools of social and emotional validation, our interactions start to feel like dueling monologues where neither party is really that interested in the other, and it's easy to walk away remembering nothing at all.

For instance, if you a share a story about a rude barista, you undoubtedly want someone to sympathize and agree that the barista was indeed being unspeakably rude. You also subconsciously want them to focus on you for a bit and cede you the spotlight. Nothing wrong with that. You're instantly less interested if someone responds that they just bought a new car, because they are keeping the spotlight on themselves and not giving you the positive feedback that we want from others.

It feels good to receive validation because it signals that other people like us.

How does this color the way you should approach interacting with other people? By keeping in mind that they want to feel heard, listened to, and acknowledged.

It seems like such an obvious truism, but now think back to the people in your daily life that can't seem to stop for one second to listen to what you have to say. People who couldn't wait for you to stop talking so they could tell you about their lives instead. The people who know nothing about you while you know the intimate details of their lives—because they never ask. Giving people positive feedback, acknowledging their emotions, and showing a listening ear are some of the biggest keys to providing validation that will make you feel liked.

Conversation Pattern #3: People are extremely lazy

You know it. I know it. People just don't want to work harder than they have to. It's a bad habit, and sometimes we are aware of it. Most of the time, however, we are not, and this translates into approaching life and others in a completely passive manner.

We typically choose the path of least resistance in life, and inertia is one of our biggest downfalls. When we hit obstacles, it is usually easier to make up an excuse and turn around and go back the way we came. Sooner or later, these become normalized habits that you can readily accept.

Sure, when we see that we can stand to benefit, we might be suddenly highly motivated to act, but otherwise, we are mostly content to let the chips fall where they may. This applies very neatly to conversation. When we're not aware of our tendency to reach for the lowest hanging fruit and be lazy, we give one-word answers, we don't show conversational initiative, and we let silences linger when they don't have to.

Worst of all, people tend to put the burden of the conversation on their conversation partner when they're lazy.

What happens when you don't ask questions, you don't engage, you don't give full answers, and you are content to let the other person dictate the conversation? Your conversation partner will have to do all of the heavy lifting with minimal input from you. It's excruciating, tiring, and quite boring overall for them. You present yourself as a dullard who delights in awkward silences, and they will see no compelling reason to interact with you again. It's like trying to have an engaging conversation with a wall—except if they were speaking to a wall, they would have proper expectations. Many of us are unknowing walls.

People are lazy conversationalists even when they don't realize it, and this also means they have the subconscious expectation of being entertained by someone else. It's not just for your satisfaction and edification, after all! Conversation can be a contact sport; if you want an activity you can passively participate in, head to the nearest movie theater for the latest romantic comedy.

To interact better with others, make sure you can allow *them* to be slightly lazy as well. Shoulder some of that conversational burden and make it easy for them. Ask better questions (we'll go over this), take more initiative in your topics (we'll go over this too), and overall take a more active and engaged role in the other person (yup, this too).

People are going to slowly begin to avoid you when it becomes clear that they are putting in a 100 percent effort while you are meandering around 25 percent effort. It may not even be the principle of the thing; they're just bored of you. These three patterns and everything that led to them are designed to peel back the shroud of mystery that conversations can seem to exist in. Essentially every problem you encounter in conversation, such as awkward silence or tension, comes from a misunderstanding or ignorance of conversation purposes or patterns.

If you don't manage to make someone feel entertained or simply enjoy your conversation, they'll be bored and mumble something under their breath about finding the bathroom sooner rather than later. If you ignore their emotions and continually deny them the spotlight, they are going to rightfully see you as a conversational narcissist and slink away subtly. Finally, if you make them do all the work and fill all the silences and lulls, they'll get annoyed and excuse themselves for a drink.

In a way, examining the facets of conversations is a completely novel sense of looking at social interaction. You're not interacting for interacting's sake—you are using interaction to satisfy the main purposes and patterns we have discussed in this chapter.

If someone brings up the weather, unless there is a tornado raging outside, do you think they *really* want to talk about the weather? If they are asking you about your weekend, do you think they are excited to hear about your growing relationship with your couch?

You know what people are looking for, so give it to them!

Chapter 2
Predictability
(In a Good Way)

When you think of the word "predictable" and apply it to a person, it's typically not a good trait.

Rachel is so predictable I could just cry when she brings up her cat again.

James is so predictable. He's going to cook pasta and then hit the bed before 9 p.m.

Karen is more predictable than a stopped clock. She's going to ask about my weekend and then my dog.

Those tend to sound like insults, and they just might be. But as the previous chapter highlighted, predictability in conversation is a good thing.

Recall the flow of:

Purpose and main interest $\rightarrow$ preparation $\rightarrow$ less anxiety $\rightarrow$ better conversations.

The previous chapter defined the first aspect: the purpose and main interests people have for social conversations. These included things like validation, entertainment, self-interest, and laziness. This chapter focuses on the second portion. Now that we understand what people are looking for, how can we adequately prepare before any conversation so we can walk in feeling like we aren't winging it completely?

I mentioned earlier that in a job interview, the epitome of the predictable conversation, you already know the main purpose and key points of discussion. In fact, if you did your due diligence, you would know the first five to ten questions you would be asked, and have amazing answers prepared for those questions. Even if the questions weren't exactly what you might expect, your answers would still educate and persuade the interviewer about your virtues and talents and fulfill the main purpose of the talk.

The parallels are clear, but I'll lay them out. You now know what people are generally looking for in social conversation, and you also know the first ten topics that will come out of someone's mouth, whether they are a stranger or old friend. Therefore, you already *know* what will come up, and *how* to address it.

It seems like I've entirely skipped the middle step of knowing the first ten topics people will speak about, but I didn't skip it—you just already have the answer to this. It's no secret or puzzle.

Just replay the most recent conversation you had with someone you met at a networking event, or even your co-worker in the break room. These are the questions we commonly categorize as small talk because they are used to fill the space and as a sort of social ritual of politeness.

- *How is your day going?*
- *How was your weekend?*
- *How is your week going?*
- *How is work?*
- *How is your family?*
- *What do you have planned for this upcoming weekend?*
- *Hey, did you hear about [current event]?*
- *Crazy about [current event], huh?*

And the tried and true, *Hey, how are you?*

So as I said, you already know what is going to come up, so it's up to you now to prepare to address these topics through the lens of the purpose and patterns of entertainment, pleasure, laziness, and validation and not let them pass by in an exchange of "Good, how about you?"

Since each of these questions, and more that you can think of, are the beginning foundations for 90 percent of all conversations, it becomes predictable, in a good way.

The best way to take advantage of this predictability is to construct engaging answers and mini stories to respond to each of the generic small talk questions. This makes logical sense, but then we instantly run into the obstacle of, "How can I answer this generic small talk question in a way that isn't also generic?"

Indeed, if you happen to be in the middle of baking a cake for your grandmother or some other out-of-the-ordinary activity, you'll have an easy way to answer most of those questions. But what if it's just a normal day during which nothing exceptional or interesting is happening?

Engaging Answers

This is where the knowledge we've accumulated about people's patterns and goals comes into play and lets you feel prepared and ready. *People don't care about the literal answers to their questions.* **This is almost always true.** They couldn't care less and are just begging to hear something that they will care about.

Do *you* care when you ask about someone's weekend? Often, we use small talk as a replacement for a salutation. It's usually just to fill the space, and the only way your ears will perk up and you will actually pay attention is the 5 percent chance that someone's weekend either involves you or is actually noteworthy. Most everything else amounts to idle chatter and will be forgotten within the hour.

Aim any and all responses towards the patterns and goals you know people have: provide entertainment, make people feel good, and allow them to be lazy by giving them something substantial. Deviating from a literal answer gives you quite a bit more freedom in how you can answer and engage people. There are two main methods to answer a boring question in an engaging way and create something from nothing.

Method #1: Answer a fuzzy version of the question

This is where you pretend you were wearing headphones when someone asked you the question, and you only heard a couple of keywords from the question.

Let's use the example question of "How was your weekend?"

The fuzzy version of the question becomes, "Blah blah, weekend?" so all you really understand is the word weekend and that someone is asking about a weekend. Therefore, your answer doesn't have to be limited to the specific weekend your conversation partner was referring to. In fact, you are answering the question but substituting it with information or a story about any notable weekend in your memory.

> Jim: How was your weekend?
>
> Bob: Oh, I didn't do much. But I forget, did I tell you last month I spent the weekend skiing and I almost broke my leg on the bunny slopes?

Instead of giving a literal answer such as, "Well, I ate a lot of Cheetos and watched *Star Trek*," Bob simply answered *something* about *a* weekend, which creates a far more interesting and engaging jumping off point for both parties. We've all had interesting weekends at some point, so it's fine to bring a more noteworthy one up in the name of entertainment. It can be a weekend from the past or the future, as long as it is something the other person would be interested in.

You can go a step further and provide a mini story about your fuzzy weekend, which you can think of as the opposite of a one-word answer. An effective mini story (per my definition anyway) contains at least five distinct details conveyed within two to three sentences—that's it. It should be no longer than fifteen to twenty seconds, and the purpose of giving a mini story is to give details that people can relate to or become curious about.

To create a mini story here, Bob could simply have added a few more details.

> Jim: How was your weekend?
>
> Bob: Oh, I didn't do much. But I forget, did I tell you last month I spent the weekend skiing and I almost

broke my leg on the bunny slopes? *I nearly went to the ER, but luckily the doctor in the ski lodge cleared me so I was able to take my wife out on our grand anniversary trip.*

Method #2: Completely re-direct

Suppose you don't have anything interesting to say about any weekend in memory, or you just want to change the topic to something more fruitful for both of you. Again, just because someone brings up the topic of your weekend to you doesn't mean you have to stick to it, especially if you are only going to be able to muster a story about watching golf on television. *No one cares, not even the person who brought it up.*

Here's what completely re-directing sounds like so you don't have to stay mired in a topic neither of you care about. It involves a pivotal word: But.

> Jim: How was your weekend?
>
> Bob: It was good, **but . . .**
>> Did you hear about . . . the latest road construction outside our office?
>> I just heard . . .
>> Did you know . . .
>> Did you see . . .

What you plug in after the pivotal "but . . ." is your opportunity to jump into whatever topic you want that fulfills your goals. All you have to do is briefly acknowledge the question they asked, and then immediately jump into another topic. It can be a fact about yourself, an interesting current event, a recent revelation you've had, or something you are extremely excited about. You are only limited by your imagination and sense of what the other person will care about.

Again, this allows you to avoid answering the question and also arms you with a smooth segue into another topic. Sometimes we find ourselves conversationally stuck because we are too polite to stop and completely change directions, even if both people want to. This gives you a solution because it's a natural way of diving into a topic that both people will enjoy.

The best part about this is you can truly prepare this beforehand by brainstorming talking points you've recently read about or learned. No more talking about the weather for ten minutes and how you both agree that rain is bad and that you both enjoy the sunshine. Move on immediately and engage on something both people will enjoy.

Of course, you can go a step further and introduce a mini story here as well. It functions the same way; you just need at least five distinct details for people to latch onto. You can include the context of your new topic and how you came upon the knowledge.

Jim: How was your weekend?

Bob: It was good, but did you hear about the latest road construction outside our office? I just read about it online and it's supposed to take a few years and cost the city millions of dollars. Apparently it's part of the new mayor's initiative for infrastructure. Couldn't we just fill the potholes ourselves with $50 and some shovels?

These two methods may seem insignificant, but let's review why they matter so much. If you take what people say at face value, and give them a literal answer, you are destined to remain in shallow small talk mode. These methods allow you to go beyond small talk while still being entertaining, validating their question, and making it easy for them to be lazy because you've just given them a great and full answer. Best of all, they allow you to prepare beforehand so you don't have to think on your feet in the heat of a conversation, when your mind is likely to go black as opposed to strike genius.

Each conversation is a blank slate for you to put your mark on. When you can prepare beforehand, you can hit the ground running and also make sure you present yourself exactly as you want, just like in a job interview.

Now that you understand how to jump into the driver's seat, there's an added benefit to taking charge. Do you want to present yourself as an outdoorsy person, or perhaps a caring and generous Samaritan? You can tailor and mold your responses to those topics so people will only see the *you* that you want them to.

Generally, understanding that there are ways of preparing for conversation beforehand will lead you to quite simply require more information about yourself. Even though you have the tools and methods to take conversations beyond small talk, you need to walk into a conversation with information ready to use, and not hidden in the attic of your brain.

The Conversation Resume

This is a concept I like to call the Conversation Resume.

The Conversation Resume isn't necessarily a checklist of things you should be bringing up in conversation, but it's an inventory of interesting information you *can* bring up in conversation to make it more personal, colorful, and interesting. Just as you are going to take stock of occurrences when you showed leadership for a job interview, you will do the same for your social conversations.

Going over your resume and updating it periodically, just as you would a job resume, will remind you that you are far more interesting than you think, you just have to remember to display it to other people occasionally. We all fall prey to feeling boring if we're bored, but it's because we allow ourselves to forget what we've done and seen.

What does the Conversation Resume include?

- Ten most notable accomplishments
- Five most unique experiences
- Activities involved in your hobbies
- Ten places you have traveled in the past three years
- Ten recent funny occurrences from your daily life
- Your life story: where you grew up and how you came to live where you live and do what you do
- What do you like to do for fun?
- What's your biggest passion?
- Where are you from?
- How long have you lived/worked here?
- Where did you go to school?
- What do you do for work?
- Pet peeves
- Favorite movies, music, and so on
- Your work history
- Ten strengths and weaknesses, no matter how small and insignificant

- Ten of your most favorite things, objects, or concepts
- Ten of your least favorite things, objects, or concepts

Most of the items on the resume are facts about yourself that exist, but aren't readily available on the tip of your tongue. Constructing your Conversation Resume does require a bit of work, but it's important to realize that if you walk into a conversation as a blank slate, then that's exactly the type of impression you will make on people.

One of the most significant sources of information you must begin to visualize is the *timelines of your life*. Take stock of yourself in the following five timelines:

The far past (previous month, year)
The near past (previous week)
The present
The near future (next week)
The far future (next month, year)

In other words, can you name any events, plans, or notable occurrences from any of those timelines? Last year, what was the most interesting thing you did, where did you travel, who did you see, and what happened to you? What plans do you have for next year, personal or professional?

What are the top five current events of the week and month? Learn the basics and develop an opinion and stance on them.

What are four funny situations from the past week? Be able to summarize them, relate them as a short story, and solicit an opinion from others.

What are the four most interesting things you've read or heard about in the past week? These can be articles or interpersonal situations from friends, work, etc. Be able to summarize them, relate them as a short story, and solicit an opinion from others.

This is the information that shows your personality and lets other people feel like they know you. It gives context and detail about your life and makes escaping small talk easy. If brainstorming this information was difficult, that's a sign that you probably aren't successfully engaging others in conversation, or at least not as well as you could.

Since this chapter is all about using predictability and the ability to prepare for conversations before the fact, there is one more trick I want to share that you can carry in your back pocket to any conversation or any time you hit an awkward silence. It's called the fallback story.

The Fallback Story

As the name implies, a fallback story is something you can prepare beforehand and use at any time with no transition or context needed. You can use it to start a conversation, or you can use it to fill a lull or silence. Think of it like a flame thrower used to erase past mistakes and create a clean slate. Interestingly, the fallback story is not focused on the story itself as much as the discussion that it creates afterwards. The fallback story has four components, and here's what it sounds like:

1. Hey, so a friend just told me . . .
2. She proposed to her boyfriend. The female proposed to the male after dating for four years.

3. I thought it was odd but I support it because why not, it's not 1950 anymore and I like to think I'm open-minded!
4. What do you think about it? Would you do this or accept that from your significant other? Have you heard about it before? How would you react?

Now let's deconstruct it.

Step one is the bridging sentence, which lets you feel like you can bring it up anytime without a transition. The primary bridging sentence here is "a friend just told me," which signals a new topic.

Step two is the actual story portion, and as you can see, here it's only one short sentence. This is because while the story itself is interesting, a story in itself does not foster discussion or conversation. It's how you frame the story and make people relate to it that does.

Step three is where you provide your opinion on the matter. You do this first so the other person feels more comfortable revealing their opinion later without a fear of judgment.

Step four is where the magic happens. You've presented an interesting premise, and now it's time to make a discussion out of it. You are soliciting their opinion in numerous ways to make sure they have something to answer and reply to.

The significance of the fallback is that you can use it as a conversational energy boost whenever you need it. If you choose the story correctly, you are going to come up with a topic that everyone has something to say about. You are creating a discussion about something inherently interesting out of thin air.

Relatability is key with fallback stories because the discussion is what matters, so they need to have some sort of opinion on it. If you use a topic that, while interesting, the other person has no concept of or context for, you can't expect any type of meaningful discussion on it. For example, if you bring up a sport that they've never even heard of, you're going to get an answer of, "Oh, that's interesting."

So where do you look? You might feel that it's tough to find topics on which everyone has an opinion besides current events (and I don't recommend using those), but you need only look as far as your relationships and the issues you may have had.

Interpersonal issues are something people almost always have an opinion on, whether positive or negative. I'm talking about all the juicy drama that sometimes happens between people. Sometimes, they even interject their opinions in an unsolicited manner. Interpersonal issues are gold because people can't resist the temptation of weighing in and handing down judgment on others.

Here's another example of an interpersonal fallback story:

A friend just told me . . .

Her boyfriend wants to get rid of her dog, a golden retriever she's had since before she met him.

I was shocked because her boyfriend knew the dog was a package deal with her, and it's totally unfair for him to change her mind. The dog is family!

What do you think? Would you ever make that kind of sacrifice? What's a deal breaker to you? Where would you draw the line on compromise?

See, now that's just a juicy situation that would probably evoke outrage in you, and you wouldn't be able to contain yourself from reacting to it. Fallback stories are short yet inflammatory in all the best ways, and they can serve you well.

This chapter was about how you can take advantage of how conversations are generally predictable to prepare statements, stories, and information beforehand to shine. You don't need to become an encyclopedia, but it certainly helps to simply know what you plan to do over the summer, remember what you did last weekend, and package these things in a way that entertain, validate, and make conversation easy for others.

It may seem like you're doing all the work and acting like a dancing monkey to entertain others. Why should you have to do the heavy lifting? Well, someone has to take the first step.

Chapter 3
The Connecting Attitude

It's time to face the simple truth: small talk is a terrible notion, invented by civil societies to inflict politeness and act as the default manner of interaction to let others know that we are indeed polite. If you asked a hundred people how they felt about small talk, at least ninety-nine would say that they hate it.

And surprisingly, despite what I teach and write about, I would absolutely be right there in the 99 percent. I'm not a fan of small talk because it can be so shallow and fake.

It's shallow because it's everyone's instinct to engage on something neutral and inoffensive to all. It also has to be relatable to everyone, and it has to be something simple. There are actually a lot of restrictions people put on what they use in small talk, so it necessarily ends up being about topics that neither party really cares about, but neither party can get upset about, the latter of which is the ultimate goal.

People also tend to swim through the shallow waters of multiple topics in short succession, which demonstrates a certain disinterest in engaging or actually listening to the answer to their questions.

It's fake because most of the time, it's clear that people are simply going through the motions and prefer small talk to silence. Small talk is the new salutation, and the ritual of asking about someone's weekend is the new showing of politeness and acknowledgment as opposed to a nod and wave.

Small talk: it's like the vegetables of friendly conversation. You may not like it, but you have to get through it to get to the good parts.

Incidentally, this is why we may not mind small talk in elevators or when we're standing in a short grocery line—we know there will be a definite end to our suffering and we see the light at the end of the tunnel. The small talk has a limit, and the limit is salvation. But when someone sidles up to the table next to us at a café and acts as if your lukewarm smile is an invitation to talk at length, we are silently screaming.

Unfortunately, this understandably negative attitude towards small talk will usually contribute to you executing it poorly and shutting your doors left and right. When you think something is unnecessary and fake, you're going to treat it as such and put in the minimal amount of fake, veneer-y effort.

Yet, small talk is the ultimate gatekeeper that we must pass through to gain friendship, rapport, and that elusive feeling of interpersonal spark. How can we turn the need to eat our conversational vegetables into something that we both enjoy and are great at?

WWJD?

It all starts with the approach and attitude we carry towards small talk and conversation at large. We are essentially asking the question of how to be more interested in other people.

This approach was summed up best by the inimitable Dale Carnegie: "You can make more friends in two months by becoming truly interested in other people than you can in two years by trying to get other people interested in you."

The implication is that when people can sense that you care and are interested in them, they will respond in kind and open up. I've found, through years of clients, the best way to articulate this is to picture your favorite talk show host. For the sake of this exercise, let's say it was Jay Leno when he was still ruling the airwaves. WWJD: What Would Jay Do?

Let's think about how he engages with guests as a talk show host.

First visualize his studio. He's got a big open space, and he is seated at a desk. There is one more chair on the other side of the desk, and despite the big room, it's like he only notices the person sitting next to him. That guest is the center of his world for the next ten minutes.

They are the most interesting person Jay has ever come across; everything they say is spellbinding, he is insatiably curious about their stories, and he reacts to anything they say with an uproarious laugh and otherwise exaggerated reaction that they were seeking. He is charmingly positive, and can always find a humorous spin on a negative aspect of a story. Jay also does the heavy lifting for his guest and segues effortlessly between topics and stories, elicits more information, finds the funny in their stories, and actually adds to them to effectuate their intent.

Jay's sole purpose is to make his guest comfortable on the show, make them talk about themselves, and ultimately make them feel good and look good. He is their biggest cheerleader and supporting actor, and this has a stunning effect on how his guest takes to him. This makes them share revealing things they might not otherwise, and create a connection and chemistry with him that is so important for a talk show. The viewers at home can tell in an instant if either party is phoning it in or faking it, so his job literally depends on his ability to connect on a deeper level.

Even with grumpy or quieter guests, he is able to elevate their energy levels simply by being intensely interested in them and encouraging them by giving them the great reactions that they seek.

The message here is that *you* are a large part of the reason you are disinterested in people or unable to see the value they can provide you with. When you act in a standoffish way because you think someone is boring or useless, they will indeed become that to you because you don't give them any chance to shine. It's the dark side of the law of attraction—when you create the reality you have in your mind.

Making a decision to be genuinely curious and interested in your conversation partner is one of the keys to allowing them to feel comfortable enough to connect to you beyond a superficial level. So even if you have to fake that type of curiosity and enthusiasm 'til you make it, WWJD should be one of the first attitudes to internalize.

When you take a step back and think about it, it really shouldn't be such a huge stretch to be curious about someone, especially a stranger. If you need more convincing, take this definition from the Dictionary of Obscure Sorrows:

> Sonder [n] *the realization that each random passerby is living a life as vivid and complex as your own, and you intersect for only a brief moment populated with their own ambitions, friends, routines, worries, and inherited craziness; an epic story that continues invisibly around you like an anthill sprawling deep underground, with elaborate passageways to thousands of other lives that you'll never know existed, in which you might appear only once, as an extra sipping coffee in the background, as a blur of traffic passing on the highway, as a lighted window at dusk.*[†]

If that doesn't make you immediately curious about the life of the person you see on the bus, the barista you see every Tuesday, or the person who seems to be wandering aimlessly around a mall, then not much else will.

For every deep thought, notion, or experience you have, everyone else you are crossing paths with is also having them at the very same depth. They are not static characters in a video game where you are the main character, and their only job is to cross paths with you.

[†] http://www.dictionaryofobscuresorrows.com/post/23536922667/sonder

Having interest and curiosity in people (or the ability to simulate it) is essentially the prerequisite for building a connection. Being absent of curiosity in others also signals something you may not have realized about yourself. If you aren't curious about others, it essentially means you expect others to entertain you.

In that case, you in fact aren't interested in dialogue, you're interested in watching a movie. You actually have the expectation for the other person to instantly entertain or captivate you, without you putting forth any effort. It can be quite startling to realize that's how you are subconsciously acting with people.

Try this quick exercise to assess how you truly perceive the people you come into contact with. Try to get them to speak as much as possible about themselves, while you say as little as possible. Ask questions, encourage them to share, and refrain from interjecting your own thoughts.

Could you keep the spotlight on someone else or were you fighting the temptation to talk about yourself? Would you rather talk about your mundane weekend than hear about someone's fascinating weekend? If this exercise was difficult, it means you probably have trouble showing interest in others and allowing them to shine. It's a startling realization for people to have, but a lack of curiosity demonstrates that you just don't see any value worth spending your time on.

Your Mantras

Instead, here are a few mantras to repeat to try to keep those compulsions at bay.

I Wonder What They Are Like?

When you start to wonder about the other person, it completely changes your perspective on them. You start to actually care and grow curious about them. You become intrigued about not only their shallow traits, such as their occupation or how their day is going, but also what motivates them and what makes them act in the way they do. You want to get inside their head and see what makes them tick. It's not just about their job or birthplace, it's about how they are as a person and the parts that make up the whole, especially their personality and quirks.

Having a sense of wonder about someone is one of the most powerful mindsets you can have because it makes you want to scratch your itch. Scratching the itch of curiosity will become secondary to everything else because you simply want to know about the other person.

Suppose you had a huge sense of curiosity about computers as a child. You were probably irritating with how many questions you asked anyone that seemed to have knowledge about computers.

So now, what kind of attention span are you going to devote to computers, and what kind of questions are you going to ask? You are going to skip the small talk interview questions and get right down to the details because it's what you care and wonder about. You're going to keep asking why, how, and where. Keeping the mindset of wonderment and curiosity will completely change the way you interact with people because you will suddenly care about knowing them, and much of the time, we don't notice that we don't care about the person we are talking to.

You can imagine how that negatively influences your conversations.

What Can They Teach Me?

Don't read this from the perspective of attempting to gain what you can from someone. Read it from the perspective of seeing others as being people worthy of your attention. Everyone has valuable knowledge, whether it applies to your life or not. Everyone is great at something, and everyone is an expert in something that you are not intimately familiar with. Thus, everyone indeed has something to teach you.

The main point is to ignite an interest in the other person as opposed to an apathetic approach. Imagine if you were a huge skiing junkie, and you met someone who used to be a professional skier. They may have even reached the Olympics in their prime.

What will follow? First, you'll be thrilled by what you can potentially learn and gain from the other person, and that will guide the entire interaction. Again, there will be a level of interest and engagement if you view others as worthy of talking to. This is a line of inquiry or even conversation that wouldn't happen if you weren't open to the possibility of people measuring up to your standards.

Whether we like to admit it or not, sometimes we feel some people are not worth our time. It's a bad habit, and this line of thinking is one of the first steps towards breaking it. If you don't probe people, you might never discover what makes them interesting and valuable, and that's your fault. Again, you're expecting someone to act as your jester instead of engaging with them.

What Do We Have in Common?

This is where you take on the mindset of Sherlock Holmes to investigate what similarities you share and what interests you have in common. Imagine you are conducting a scavenger hunt, and you are tasked with interviewing people to discover their favorite kind of snack. This gives you a reason to be engaged with someone.

You are going to be on a hunt, and you will thus ask the important questions that get you where you want to be. You might jump from topic to topic, or you might dive in and ask directly. When you have something else to focus on besides interacting for interaction's sake, conversation flows much better.

The best part is what happens when you finally discover the obscure or huge commonality you share. Just imagine that you broke your left arm when you were eight years old, and they did the same. Now imagine what how you will feel about them, and where the conversation will naturally flow after that discovery. Again, these are the types of high points you're denying if you don't actively take interest in others.

What's Unique about Them?

Everyone has some sort of claim to fame or obscure talent they happen to excel at. Make it your job to find it. Whether this means asking about someone's talents, hobbies, interests, or background, make it happen.

A big reason we don't engage with others is because we think there is nothing below the surface level, that their exteriors hold all that there is to know about them. Of course, this is untrue because human beings are much closer to icebergs than anything else. Even with the most gregarious or expressive of us, the vast majority of our thoughts will still be internal. The only way to discover them is to engage and ask.

The purpose of these four mantras is twofold. First, they serve to realize that others are far more than you give them credit for, and second, they ignite a sense of curiosity that will drive conversation and even overpower a sense of boredom and false superiority. These attitudes drastically change how you approach people, and subsequently what you talk about with them.

We're not always the best at everything we try our hand at, and we're not all that and a bag of chips. Other people have at least five things that they can teach us in a pinch. We also inevitably share commonalities with others, even though it may be below the surface. So it's really not a stretch to believe these mantras.

Make it your mission to find those things and gain value from others, as well as impart your own. If you don't actually think that other people are interesting or can provide you anything of value (be it just information or entertainment), then you are likely to act that way and not establish any sort of connection.

Buzzkills

Some attitudes are detrimental to connecting with others: If you don't think they are worth your time, such as if you are just talking to them to kill time, or if you immediately write them off as boring or knowing nothing of value.

First of all, as we discussed, if that's how you view someone, the failure is on you for not being able to see what is unique and interesting about them.

Second, if you see someone as lesser than you, it means you see yourself as better and more interesting than them. Just think for a second about the type of person who constantly thinks this about the people they come across. Does it sound like the type of person you'd like to spend time with? Probably not, which means even you wouldn't want to spend time with yourself.

Finally, it means you expect others to entertain and cater to you. You don't feel like you need to lift a finger, and others should captivate you and keep you entertained like a court jester. In other words, you subconsciously want a great conversation without doing any of the work yourself. You want to watch a movie, not participate in a dialogue.

However difficult it is to admit, our attitudes surrounding others significantly impede our ability to connect with them. Everyone is worth your time, and no one is inherently beneath you. Do you truly believe that, or do you only light up when someone appears to be able to offer you something in return?

The next time you go out to a café or store, put these attitudes to the test with the captive audience of the baristas or cashiers you come across, the lucky few who are paid to be nice to you.

Do you perceive these workers to be below you, do you treat them differently than you would a good friend? Or do you have a sense of wonderment and curiosity about them? What do you think they can teach you, and what do you have in common with them?

These are levels of thought we might reach if we meet someone who is clearly superior to us in our career, but we ignore these levels of care for everyone else. Do you tend to ask the baristas or cashiers about their day and actually care about their answer? If not, do you think you'll be able to simply "turn it on" when you're around people you care about?

The mindsets for connection are things you have to practice. You can't regard a barista or cashier in one way, then turn into another person for VIPs only. Achieving this level of caring and interest in the people around you is what makes you able to connect with anyone in sixty seconds or less, and it's something that happens when you live it, not just pick and choose to use it. Practice this level of caring and interest by attempting to get to know the people who are serving you at your favorite café or ringing you up at the cash register. You will be pleasantly surprised by what you find, and it will expose you to what you've been blinding yourself to.

Overall, prioritize the other person and avoid social narcissism. If your favorite topic of conversation is yourself and your own life, you just might be a social narcissist. If you listen only to wait for your turn to speak again, don't care about other people's lives, or even ask about people's days, you just might be a social narcissist.

This chapter is a long-winded way of extolling the benefits of being genuinely open-minded and how it can benefit the connections you are able to make.

Chapter 4
Break the Ice with Anyone

To many people, breaking the ice and starting a conversation seems like attempting to scale a boulder.

It's why many people feel destined to become wallflowers, or feel lonely within a group of people. Others might be within poking distance, but how can you penetrate their aura or conversation without coming off as a—well, you can fill in the blank here. Imagine standing around at a networking event or party, and thinking about the prospect of breaking into one of the pre-existing groups. They might as well have force fields around them that keep people like *you* out.

Inevitably, we come up with a veritable laundry list of excuses why we can't do it.

- They look so busy.
- I don't want to interrupt them.
- I'll be too awkward.
- I don't want to seem weird.

So while breaking the ice is in reality a very simple act, we make it far more difficult on ourselves because we attach such a huge stigma to simply talking to a stranger out of the blue. It represents a rejection on a very personal level because we know people will be looking at us, sizing us up, and saying yes or no based on what they see.

That's not necessarily true, but the possibility of it being true is large enough to keep us firmly rooted in place and spouting the excuses from above that allow us to stay there. They're almost textbook defense mechanisms that allow us to not act, which allows us to not put ourselves on the line for rejection and judgment.

The first step to breaking the ice is the ability to step up to the plate. That was one metaphor too many for one sentence, but the point is that we first have to deal with the defense mechanisms that keep you from acting.

One of the first ways is to give yourself a social goal.

Social Goals

I like going to the beach on occasion, but I don't like staying there for extended periods of time. It might just be how I'm wired, but laying in the sun just isn't my idea of an ideal day.

I like the sun and the water, but the part about the beach I don't like is that it feels like there is no purpose to it. Now, on the other hand, I'd be thrilled to go to the beach to play volleyball or to catch an amazing sunset view. I would have a clear reason to be there and it would make it more fulfilling for me. It would actually make me excited about it and not just counting down the minutes until I leave.

It's tough to break into a conversation with someone when it feels like that's your main purpose, and you are socializing just to socialize. It's too easy to talk yourself out of it.

But having a social goal can give you the motivation and excuse to push through your defense mechanisms in pursuit of that goal. It essentially provides us plausible deniability, which is the ability to say, "I had a perfectly reasonable excuse for doing this, so don't mind me!" which allows us to sidestep that looming fear of judgment and rejection.

Suppose your car breaks down, and the only way you can escape your situation is to flag down another car and charm them into letting you use their phone and tire iron. It would require no little amount of small talk and social interaction, especially if you convince them to give you a ride to the nearest gas station.

Would breaking the ice be a problem in that situation? No, because you had an overarching goal that made everything else essentially irrelevant. Your social defense mechanisms were overridden by the necessity of fixing your car. You had something you needed to accomplish, and you were able to push through to it no matter how tired you were.

That's the power of having a social goal. It makes fear and rejection secondary and allows you to break the ice. If you dread networking events, you can still make them productive and useful if you set yourself a clear social goal and/or have a dire reason for engaging with people. The prospect of blindly stumbling around a networking event is daunting, but going in with something to accomplish provides clear focus and motivation.

We are, after all, creatures of pleasure. We tend to run away from pain and toward comfort. With the process of setting upfront goals that will focus your social efforts, you may not be able to increase the pleasure you get from social interaction, but you will be able to decrease the associated pain.

There are two types of social goals you can mentally keep to create plausible deniability for yourself and conquer those nagging fears of judgment and rejection.

The Sherlock Holmes Goal

It's fairly rare that we take a true interest in other people. It's a shame, but it's reality. Unless we have a large shared interest, or we know some of the same people, most people are just ships that pass by in the night and we take a similar amount of interest.

It's not always a bad thing. It's what humans require to function on a day to day basis and focus on our priorities.

This goal sounds easy, but it is not something we always do. Sherlock Holmes, the famous literary detective, would use his powerful skills of deduction through asking questions and making observations. The Sherlock Holmes goal is to do the same and make it your goal to learn as much about other people, make observations about them, and put them all together in a few assumptions.

Ask as many questions as you can, ask about your observations, and test your assumptions by asking them about those. Use your sense of curiosity and try to find what's interesting about people you meet.

Don't just small talk people—learn about them!

Game Goals

A game goal is just what it sounds like. When you're playing a video game, what is the biggest motivation to do better and keep trying at it? The score, be that getting a high score, beating other people's scores, or just achieving a score.

This social goal brings it to real life. When you're at a networking event, for example, a game goal would be to collect ten business cards in the next hour, or even to see how many business cards you can get during the whole event.

Other examples would be learning everyone's first name and place of birth at a party, or verbally maneuvering an opening to tell that one story of yours to at least two different people.

Additional examples could be successfully getting some fresh air outside with two separate people, exchanging social media accounts with three people, or learning an embarrassing story about four people that night.

See how these game goals can energize and focus your efforts, instead of simply making small talk and hoping it goes somewhere? They keep you entertained through having an ulterior motive and generally keep you invested in other people. That's really the idea with social goals—to continue caring about other people when you just feel tired inside.

Social interaction is like working out. Goals are like steroids that enable more gym time, and that let your social muscles blossom like a combination of the Hulk and Arnold Schwarzenegger. Inject some steroids (goals) into your muscles, and see how strong you can build your battery.

Does this mean it is completely pain-free? Not at all, even with the steroid of goals. You still have to put in the work, and nothing is ever gifted to you. The first few times might be absolute nightmares. In many cases, you might even feel as if you want to throw up or run out of the nightclub or bar . . . yes, even if you have an overarching goal.

In a way breaking the ice mirrors how we feel about conversation at large. We need to feel comfortable enough to engage, and then know what to say after we're in the situation. Hopefully we have taken care of the first part, and now we are left with the question of what to actually say.

Four Types of Icebreakers

There are four main types of icebreakers you can use to begin speaking with anyone. Notably, they give us the same feeling of protection and plausible deniability that social goals give us.

In reality, there are only three to teach because you already know the fourth method, which is directly going up to someone and saying, "Hello, how are you? My name is _____." We are going through these methods precisely because that is outside most people's comfort zones.

So the first of the three real types of icebreakers occurs when you ask someone for their subjective opinion. Let's use the example of speaking to a stranger at a party. When you ask for a subjective opinion, your social goal is to discover the information. You have plausible deniability because you're not trying to interact with them to become their friend, you are just taking an opening to find something out that you need to know.

For example, you might turn to the person next to you and ask, "Hey, what do you think of the music here? I'm thinking about having a party next weekend and am still building my playlist."

This is a much easier way to approach someone because you are simply curious about something and want a second opinion. You are also inviting someone to share their opinion, which people are happy to do, especially if it is on something they care about. There's no wrong answer here, and that makes it easier for both of you when you are breaking the ice.

The second method is to ask for objective information. We can go back to the example of speaking to a stranger at a party. Asking for objective information is when you seem to require information, and any source will do. Imagine asking someone for the time, or the location of the nearest café. Or: "Hey, do you know where the host of the party is?"

Something as simple as that is objective information, where you are just asking a question as plainly as possible, and allowing people to answer and help you. Again, you can use this in just about any type of situation because it's innocent and doesn't imply anything on your part.

The final type of icebreaker is to comment on a shared reality. A shared reality is something about the environment that is either observable or known on an unspoken level. It has to be relatable, and the other person has to immediately understand the context behind it. This is easy to use because, again, it's not directly attempting to start a conversation, which you might be uncomfortable with.

For example, commenting on a shared reality is leaning over your shoulder and saying within earshot of someone else, "Can you believe the tone of this music? I think the word I'm looking for is 'spatial.'"

You're making an observation about the environment you are both in and expressing your opinion on it. The other person is also exposed to it, so they likely will be able to form some type of opinion on it. Regardless, the plausible deniability here is that something is so notable you can't help but comment on it out loud.

"Hey, is it just me or does the music here remind you of a 1970s disco club?"

The problem many people run into with these icebreaking methods is they feel like they can't come up with questions to ask others, or that they don't need any objective information, or aren't wondering about anyone's subjective opinion.

It may require you to be more observant and aware of the elements that are around you, but remember that that portion of the conversation will last roughly two seconds, so feel free to ask people questions you already know the answer to, or something you don't need an opinion on just to break the ice. The goal is to begin engaging with someone, not to actually gain knowledge—remember, that's your plausible deniability speaking.

Above all else, these methods—social goals, subjective opinions, and objective information—they get you right past the fear of rejection and judgment because you are initially engaging in a way that is completely devoid of them. Will someone judge you if you ask for what time it is, or where the party is located? Are you at risk for rejection if you ask whether someone likes the décor or where how much they think the beer cost?

So you are able to circumvent the scary part of breaking the ice and jump right into a conversation. You have gotten their attention in an indirect and innocent way, then engage as normally afterwards. This cures the problem of what to say and gives you an in to anyone in any situation and gives you an excuse to interrupt them.

Remember the car example from earlier—these are just everyday versions that you can implement in your life.

Now that you know what to say, it's equally important to say it in a way that will create the best results.

Warming Up

Not temperature-wise like a hot dog in the microwave, but more like a muscle before a Zumba class. You can't just walk into a big party straight from waking up from a long nap.

What happens when you try to do that? You'll stutter, your mind will be blank, and you'll have to keep clearing your throat because your vocal cords will be asleep still.

You need to warm up, get in the zone, and get ready to socialize.

Social skills are muscles that you need to stretch before vigorous use, and ignoring that fact will just ensure that you don't utilize your full potential. If you don't, you'll spend your first three conversations warming up and you definitely won't be as quick-witted or charming as you would like.

Athletes warm up and stretch before a big game, so you should too. Social muscles are like any other muscle, so warming up beforehand can help you hit the ground running. Otherwise you will take the first conversation to warm up and you will bungle it. This is why some people do pushups or scream before they go on stage to speak to a crowd, for example. They're preparing themselves mentally and physically to make sure their "A" game comes out.

Some people will use external stimuli such as loud music and motivational videos (like the president's speech in the movie *Independence Day* before the pilots take on the alien army), but my favorite way is a little bit more direct.

Here's what you're going to do. Find a passage, preferably from a children's book or something with dialogue that has (1) different characters and (2) a variety of emotions. Or you can just use the dialogue I have for you below. The greater the diversity of the text you are reading, the more warmed up you will be. After all, runners don't just jog and call it a day for warming up. They do various exercises targeted towards optimally warming up different parts of their body for performance.

Pretend you're a grade-school teacher reading to your classroom and read out loud. Exaggerate all the emotions, and be as hyperbolic as possible. Be loud, shout, and make crazy hand gestures. Assign characters and voices to each part and act them out as vividly as possible. Be outlandish to the point of feeling embarrassed and silly, even though no one can hear you.

Scream parts of it loudly, while whispering other parts. Use different and zany voices for different characters. Exaggerate any emotion you see in the excerpt tenfold, be it insane laughter, boiling rage, confusion, joy, etc.

Read the excerpt like you're giving a performance in a contest, and the winner is judged on how emotional and ridiculous they can be! Or, pretend you're a voice actor for a movie trailer, and you have only your voice to get a wide range of emotion across.

For example, try reading the following three times. Try to push your limits and do each time more ridiculous and outlandish than the prior reading.

> **Sad Donkey**: You know, it's so sad that the lamb has to leave early. I really enjoyed spending time with him, and I'm just going to miss him so much!
>
> **Mischievous Cat**: Oh, I can't imagine why the lamb has to go now. I really have no idea what could have happened. I'm sad just like you are. Why wouldn't I be?
>
> **Dopey Dog**: Hey guys, where are we going after? Can we go to the park? I really enjoy the park and running around out there. Did you know there's a drinking fountain there now?
>
> **Shy Lamb**: Gosh, I'm just—Oh, I don't know. I can't. The park sounds fun but I just don't know. What about staying inside quietly with a movie?
>
> **Ecstatic Elephant**: I'm so happy and thrilled that lamb is leaving. I like him but he will be onto bigger and better things. Not bigger than me of course. It's time to celebrate with a cocktail in everyone's trunk and a party hat if it fits you. Mine doesn't.

Notice the difference between the first and third time, just in that short span of time? That's the difference between how you appear at a party without warming up versus warmed up. It's a difference with a huge effect on the impressions you make.

This also increases your ability to show and express emotions because you are pushing the range of emotions you express and becoming used to the exaggerated versions—which to other people might just appear normal. It's like breaking the dam and letting the waterfall of emotions flow. If you tend to use a monotone voice or lack vocal expressivity, reading out loud in this particular manner will help you create a consistent message and make no ambiguity for what you are thinking inside.

But uh oh, what if you're in too deep and you find out you are conversing with a conversational narcissist whose goal for the night seems to be to talk your ear off?

What if you've done the unthinkable—broken the ice too effectively? Then you're going to need an escape formula.

Conversation Escape Formula

The conversation escape formula is how you can leave any interaction any time you want without waiting for the other person to tire of talking.

In reality, this is as easy as interrupting someone abruptly and saying that you need to leave, but we never want to do that for fear of feeling awkward. Actually, we want to spare the other person the feelings of judgment and rejection we so fear ourselves.

However, it just takes four steps to gain your freedom while sparing people's feelings.

First, have an excuse ready to leave any conversation or social situation. Using the bathroom, needing to call someone, or searching for someone else almost always works. It doesn't have to be too specific, just have something ready on the tip of your tongue.

Second, act as if the need for an exit is urgent, so the other people in your context won't take it personally or question it. This is important because we sometimes feel that leaving a conversation is tantamount to rejecting someone. In a way, it is, but we can mask that feeling by conveying urgency and importance. No one is going to feel insulted if you need to go home because your apartment is flooding.

Third, ask for permission and then apologize for having to leave. This drives home how genuine and courteous you are. Show remorse about the fact that you are escaping and they'll feel good about it. No one will ever refuse you permission, but this makes them recognize and appreciate the gesture.

Finally, say something about the future. For example, "Let's do this again soon" or "I want to continue this conversation!" These endings add a final level of empathy and care so people can feel good about the fact that you are departing.

As you can see, most of these factors are aimed towards obscuring the fact that you simply don't want to be there anymore, and sparing the feelings of the other people. You are conveying your full message, but without the negative impact.

These four steps can help you build an exit strategy for wherever you go, and whatever situation you find yourself in.

Finally, what if you want to break the ice for other people? You can easily just introduce them by their names and occupations, but there's a better way that will lead to better engagement and bigger laughs.

Outrageous Introductions

When you introduce others, you should create an outrageous factor that thrusts people together. When the focus of the conversation is on anything but the other person, even momentarily, it drastically decreases the amount of pressure to constantly talk and makes it far more comfortable and natural for people.

"Candy, have you met Ben? He bikes to work in tiny spandex every day." I introduced these two with a funny fact about one of the parties, which he will feel compelled to defend and justify and tell a story about, while she pokes fun at him.

"Lisa, this is John. Last time I hung out with John, we ended up in the same bed together." I pointed out a funny commonality the parties share. He will launch into the story about ending up together, and she will laugh her head off at it.

"Angie, this is Kenneth. You both have unfortunately seen how much body hair I have." Here, I made myself the butt of the joke to be laughed at. They will probably gang up on me and share stories about how bad my body hair is, and the last time they both saw it.

"Carol, this is Charles. Carol, remember when you tore that guy's shirt off at the bar?" During this instance, I introduced a funny story about one of the parties, which she will adamantly and proudly justify while he cracks up.

"Steph, this is Andrew. I'm pretty sure you two have the most delicate stomachs ever."

I focused on a humorous commonality the two of them share, which will result in them comparing notes and experiences about it, no matter how gross. The point is to make them laugh to disarm them. Ninety-nine percent of the time when you use any of the introduction techniques in this book, there will be a related story that will kick-start their conversation. If I could sum this chapter up in one takeaway, it would be this: shift the focus away from their meeting.

A bit better than swapping occupations, hometowns, and colleges, isn't it?

Chapter 5
Avoid Being Avoided

One of my best friends never knows when to shut up.

Most of the time I enjoy this about him because he usually has something insightful or hilarious to say. He is forever a source of entertainment because he has no reservations about poking fun at every aspect of himself. He might be the most shameless person I know.

He isn't, however, a great listener.

This is showcased mostly when I want to rant about something inane that happened during my day, such as a driver cutting me off, or the market running out of my favorite kind of doughnuts (maple-glazed) before I could get there.

The only purpose for those rants is to burn off some of my annoyance so it doesn't affect the rest of my day. It doesn't take long, and I'm not screaming or pounding the table.

Despite all this, he just *has* to interject immediately and try to solve the problem. For example, if I am indeed complaining about the absence of doughnuts, he'll immediately ask me what I can do about it, and suggest five actions for me to take to find the doughnuts from either his source, or petition the market to fry more in the afternoons.

I can appreciate the gesture, but it's downright annoying when I can't finish my thought without hearing suggestions that I will never use and barely care about. Sometimes you just want to gripe a little and be heard; you are not actually looking for advice or even a solution.

Despite how great a person you might be, you probably have toxic habits that repel people instead of attract them, habits that make you an anti-people person. If "just be yourself" hasn't been working for you, then perhaps it's because "yourself" is grating, lacks tact, and doesn't play well with others. You just might have some habits that are blocking your path to greater success in all areas of your life.

There's always room for improvement, and you have to be open to letting go of some key traits that you think make up who you are.

Bad Habits

Sometimes it's just as important to know what not to do versus what to do. You could be the most delightful person and provide the exact solution people are looking for, but if you have toxic conversational habits, no one will want to hear them.

They would rather suffer than spend time with you. Think about the person in your office or social circle that exemplifies this sentiment. You'd go out of your way and in fact be willing to spend more money and waste more time just so you don't have to interact with them. If they just reformed those little habits and acts that grated on your every nerve, you might even find them charming and funny!

Simply put, you are never fully present.

When you're talking with other people, you give out the impression that you'd rather be somewhere else, with someone else. We've covered this before, but this time I want you to take the perspective that it's a terrible habit that can easily repel others.

You think in the back of your mind that other people simply are not that interesting. Frankly, you think other people are boring and aren't worth your time. It's bad enough that you think these things, but then you make it worse by telegraphing your feelings through your body language and your lack of eye contact. If you've ever spoken to someone who seems to be scanning the room for other people to speak to, this is the feeling you are giving others.

When people look at you, they can easily tell that you are not interested and in turn will think you not a nice person to be around. At best, you make people feel you simply don't care about them. At worst, you can come off as somebody who's flat-out hostile.

And you know what? It's your fault for not valuing the person in front of you enough to make an effort.

The quick fix to this bad habit is to admit that this is your fault.

If you think you're having a boring conversation that you want to get away from, you have to admit that you caused the problem. You caused the conversation to be boring because you expected it to be interesting, and you expected to be entertained by the other person instead of creating a conversation together.

How much work did you want to put in? You had a sense of entitlement, and because of your disengagement, the other person also got nothing out of the interaction.

The fix here is to realize, appreciate, and understand that it's your job to make the conversation interesting. It's your responsibility. Pretend that you are a talk show host and ask questions about them to figure out why they do the things they do. Ask questions about the opinions they hold. Make it your goal to find common ground or an interesting tidbit about their life.

This is only possible if you have a sense of curiosity about other people. And if you don't have a natural sense of curiosity about what goes on in other people's lives, fake it. Think of people you've wanted to meet since you were a child. What kind of questions would you ask them? Let people become aware of your sense of curiosity and energy and they will reciprocate. If possible, take on a child-like (not childish) sense of curiosity and single-mindedly pursue answers to questions about others. Put your phone down, stop composing answers in your head, and just focus on what was said, why it was said, and the emotions the other person is feeling.

That seems like a whole new level of analysis that will take you out of the present, but it's analysis that is focused on the other person, not on something inside your own head.

You Are a Conversational Narcissist and Dominate Conversations

Conversational narcissists don't listen; they simply wait until the other person stops talking so they can start speaking again.

They view the time during which another person is talking as a resting period for their vocal cords. It's neither intentional nor conscious; it's simply that their default mode of thinking is self-centered and about themselves. If there's a lull, they'll bring themselves back up—not because they want to hog the conversation, but because they are most preoccupied with themselves and find themselves the most interesting party in a conversation.

Others are involved, sure, but as supporting actors to react to their stories.

They might not acknowledge what others say. They might not even ask how the other person is doing. When people talk this way, whatever the cause, it shows a deep and profound lack of interest in what drives, motivates, and interests other people.

Don't be the person who takes others hostage by talking their ears off. Do you know anything about others, or do they all know the miniscule details about your life? Is there an information imbalance because you tend to bring everything back to your own thoughts? If you answered yes to either of those questions, it's because you tend to talk more and listen less.

Thankfully, there is a quick fix to this narcissistic conversational mindset: impose a limit on yourself.

For example, for every story you share, you must ask the other person two questions about the story, or about things that are important to them. Keep track internally of how self-centered you are with regards to the topics you choose to talk about.

Challenge yourself to make your conversation a game to find out as much about other people as you can while saying as little as possible about yourself or the things you find interesting. Realize that people only feel good about and enjoy a conversation when they are sharing, and you feel the same way.

Allow others to feel good by giving them time and space to talk about what's important to them. Otherwise, people will start avoiding you because they will think of you as someone who doesn't care. They might already have started to.

This narcissistic conversational habit comes from a place of insecurity and a need to prove oneself. It can get boring quite quickly. Give others air space and know that the inclination to prove oneself immediately is a dead giveaway for insecurity.

You Give Unsolicited Advice or Opinions

This is my best friend to a tee. Remember how he wouldn't let me just finish my thoughts and express my emotions?

Many times, people just want to talk about something and think out loud. They're not looking to debate, realize something profound, hear advice, or act on anything. They just want to be heard and validated in a comfortable setting. In many cases, they just want to get a weight off their chest and share feelings. If someone is telling a story about being cut off in traffic, they don't want advice on how to drive better and more safely. They just want to say their piece and get it off of their chest.

And that's it. That's all they're looking for. If people want advice, they'll ask for it specifically.

You must be able to read people so you don't immediately turn them off by ignoring these central facts. When you give a response they were not looking for, people will begin to stay away from you. They might not even realize it, just knowing that they are walking away from a conversation with you feeling unfulfilled or unsatisfied in some odd way—not realizing it's because you haven't let them express themselves.

The quick fix here is to take a split second and ask yourself a quick binary question: Does this person actually want my input, or are they just letting off steam and need an ear to scream into? There is a big difference between the two. Take a moment to ascertain the purpose of a person's statement, and you will understand what they want from you—and be able to give it to them.

If someone is asking for advice, let them ask specifically and explicitly. Otherwise, shut up. If they don't ask you for specific advice or specific solutions, be content with being a simple sounding board.

It's like going to a restaurant, and having the waiter look at you and say, "Okay, plain hamburger here." When you're at a restaurant, you should be able to make a choice for yourself instead of acting the same way to different people.

Allow people to spill their guts to you and they'll begin to trust you with other things as well.

Never Laugh First

We all have fake laughs. No matter how honest we think we are, or how much we hate sugarcoating things to people, we still utilize our fake laughs on a daily basis.

Here's the thing about most of us—we're inherently nice! We want people to like us, we want social situations to go smoothly, and we want awkward silences to die.

Most importantly, we don't want people to feel bad about themselves when they inevitably make a bad joke.

So we throw them a pity chuckle.

Fake laughter is the lubricant that salvages many conversations. It fills empty space and gives you something to do when you have no idea what to say. It keeps conversation rolling and gives the appearance of engagement even if you're bored out of your mind. Appearances, as it turns out, do matter sometimes. If you're speaking with the head honcho of your company, you know that your best fake laughter will be put to the test because you want them to like you.

And sometimes we depend on the fake laughter of other people to prevent us from feeling self-conscious or stupid.

So we laugh at people's jokes. Laughter is pretty much an integral part of our daily lexicon—but that doesn't mean we like it, and the more we have to do it with someone, the more tiring and more unpleasant it is to talk to them.

Obviously, fake laughter from others is something we want to avoid, so what is the biggest step we can take to prevent it?

Always laugh second. Never laugh first.

The biggest culprit for people to use their fake laughter and ultimately get tired of talking to you is when you laugh at your own joke loudly and proudly, and without looking to the other person for a reaction . . . especially when the jokes aren't great, time after time. Think about it.

Monica makes a mediocre joke and laughs at it. Don't you feel like you have to give her a fake chuckle to keep the conversation moving and give her the reaction she is seeking?

Okay, so you force a smile onto your face and expel some breath from your lungs. No big deal.

Then Monica does it again. And again. And again. And your facial muscles start to hurt because of how much you have to contort it into a fake, glazed-over smile.

That's what laughing at your own jokes first without gauging how the other person receives it will do to your conversation partners. When you always laugh first, you're imposing your will on the conversation partner and essentially telling them how to feel. Cumulatively, it's torture to deal with.

Another detriment to always laughing first at your own jokes is it leaves you completely unable to gauge how funny you actually are. Without any proper and uninfluenced reactions, you are living in a world where you only hear laughter—laughter of your own that you manufacture. This can lead to an inflated sense of self. I'm sure you have friends who think they are hilarious because all they do is hear their own laughter.

Others might laugh with you, but it doesn't mean they think you're funny. Always laughing first is usually a reaction born out of insecurity and the fear of conversational rejection, which is essentially silence after a joke.

Not getting the emotional reaction that you want can be embarrassing or downright paralyzing to some people, so it makes sense that they want to seed the emotion. It's understandable and we've all felt it when we were feeling shy or nervous about something, a.k.a. nervous laughter.

The quick fix here is to just stop this practice and become comfortable with the lack of reaction after you make a quip or joke. In a sense, you are becoming comfortable with silence—but it's only a slight moment of silence that you must overcome and not fill with laughter or noise. If you can mentally fill that silence inside your own mind, you will likely stop laughing first.

Belief Patrol Membership

Have you ever had that feeling that you just needed to set the record straight on something?

It might not even concern you, and it certainly doesn't affect your life. The other person also likely won't care that much. In cases like this, if you were to really think about it, it becomes fairly clear that we are only doing this for ourselves.

Why, exactly?

Because you can't stand the idea of someone believing something that you don't. In short, you are a member of the Belief Police. This causes us to spend way too much time squabbling over things that really don't move the needle just because we feel that other people believe or think something different than we do and must be corrected.

If you've ever been around a know-it-all, you know exactly what I'm talking about. If you don't, you might be a badge-carrying member of the Belief Police.

Whomever you're speaking with, there will inevitably come a point where you don't match up with them. If it's about a topic that you have a personal investment in, it's easy to get in over your head and try to win the other person to your side. You think, "How could anyone think any differently? The conclusion is so clear!"

And then we grapple with feelings of annoyance and frustration that someone has a different belief even though it doesn't touch our lives in any way.

The vast majority of the time, this kind of squabbling occurs in places like the comments sections of a YouTube video or a news blog. When you scroll down into the rabbit hole, you will see people arguing over the smallest pedantry and nitpicking for days. Mostly, the arguments are between two people who simply don't want to give up any ground. Instead of admitting any fault or wrong, they battle until they no longer remember what their actual intent or motivation was.

We feel that since we know so much better than the other person, we have some sort of responsibility to correct them. We then take it upon ourselves to prove to them just how smart we are. We just can't stand someone believing something wrong or contrary to what we believe!

These tendencies play out all the time, and in many cases they involve issues that are of very little importance. The Belief Police typically need to be right all the time.

A Belief Police Officer might be very effective at imposing their beliefs on others . . . but this habit is going to make them downright obnoxious to talk to, and not in an affectionately obnoxious kid sister kind of way. People will avoid them. Who wants to spend time with someone who makes them feel judged, attacked, and defensive?

The bottom line is that the bulk of these arguments all stem from the all-too-human tendency to "police" other people's beliefs.

Instead of saying, "Well, you could be right, that's true. You also have a point. Moving on!" you stand your ground and want to show intellectual dominance. The great part about this type of statement is you're not making an actual assertion or conceding to their position, you're just validating them and moving on.

You have to catch yourself when you slip into this mode because it is not only subtle, but also very addictive because of the payoff at the end. Let's face it, it feels amazing when someone acquiesces and says, "Yeah, you're right, I'm wrong."

But at what cost does this admission come?

If you took an aerial view of your heated conversations with your friends, co-workers, associates, and colleagues, in almost all cases you would probably conclude that almost none of it truly mattered. Your pride and ego did, but not the issue at hand.

Most of the time, the reason you have such arguments is that someone has taken on the role of Belief Police Officer. You've given yourself the job of patrolling other people's minds, assumptions, and beliefs.

What if you expressed your religious beliefs and someone couldn't stop trying to convert you to a different religion? What if you expressed your love of a certain food or drink and someone just couldn't stop telling you how disgusting it was? What if you expressed your opinion on a favorite movie or television show and someone couldn't stop telling you that you *needed* to watch other shows?

It's frustrating being the recipient of this attitude because you feel attacked, and it's not as if they are going to change your mind anyway. It's futile. So what gives you reason to think that it's not going to be unwelcome when you do it to other people? It says more about you than it does about them if you feel the need to constantly interject your opinions and thoughts. Being part of the Belief Police is for your benefit, not theirs, even though in your mind you are seeking to benefit them with your knowledge.

Follow this quick fix to break out of this behavior pattern: don't share your opinion unless asked. Unless someone has asked you for your opinion, or is quite obviously soliciting your arguments as part of a debate, don't engage them. Otherwise, all you're doing is butting in and trying to convince someone that their opinion or sense of taste is incorrect.

Err on the side of neutral. Engage momentarily just to acknowledge that they do have an opinion, but don't attempt to convince or police them.

This is especially true when it comes to matters of taste and opinion. These are completely subjective. What looks good to you might be completely ugly to another person. You won't convince anyone to like chocolate more than they already do, or to like beets when they hate them, so, it's really a waste of your time—and an extremely annoying one at that—to exert your energy trying to convince them.

The bottom line: if something is not affecting you directly, or it's a one-time occurrence and the issue is something that is near and dear to your heart, choose to resist the temptation to be the Belief Police. In fact, resist the temptation more than that.

Just let others be right (or think they are right) most of the time. Choose your battles and don't fret about the small details of what you can't change. You'll be happier and less stressed, and you'll notice a direct correlation between that and the quality of your friendships and interactions.

This habit is particularly toxic because people who have this mindset are very judgmental. When they come across people who don't fit the mold of how they feel the world should operate, they judge them, sometimes to their faces. They are prone to thinking of that person as someone who is wrong, and can only respond in a very stereotypical way.

Unfortunately, our natural selfishness tends to translate to a black and white view in such a way that when our opinions are questioned, we ourselves feel judged and attacked. So people stop opening up to you, and will eventually avoid you altogether.

Your grand explanation for something is just one possible conclusion that is neither better nor worse, just based on the information you have at your fingertips. Jog your creative faculties and try to understand how other people might have ended up with such a different opinion. Is their worldview dramatically different from yours? What experiences have they had in their lives that might explain why they hold a position in such contrast to yours? Remember that people have their own reasons for opinions and beliefs and that not everybody thinks just the way you do.

Pointless Questions

You've probably heard a lot of advice on how open-ended questions are great for getting people to talk about themselves. That's true to an extent.

However, can you come up with a quick answer for the following question: "What do you like to do for fun?"

I bet not, and there's a very good reason. It's too open-ended. It's so open-ended that it becomes vague, and when something is vague, people become confused. They aren't sure what kind of answer you are looking for, what the context is, or why you are even asking it at all.

In most cases, you're going to end up with an answer of, "Um . . . that's a good question. I'm not sure. I need to think about it. What about you?"

The truth is when you ask a general question, you will get a general answer. It's just a hard question to answer because no one thinks about their life in such broad and vague terms as "what they do for fun." Remember, you want to enable people to be lazy, and open-ended questions actually make us think quite a bit and inject lulls into conversation.

Well, what happens when you hop to the other side of the spectrum and ask an extremely specific question, such as, "What is your favorite movie of all time?"

You'll actually get the same stuttering answer as before, but for different reasons. This question is hard to answer because it is asking for one single answer, and it's an answer that you want to represent you in a positive light. So not only is it asking you to identify a movie you like, but a movie that you think others might like, be able to relate to, and will sound good to others. When you ask extremely specific questions, they actually make you pause because you need to ensure that your answer is optimal and makes you look good in the face of judgment.

And of course, it's just not easy to think of a single movie sometimes.

As you can see, both ends of the spectrum—specific and broad—are detrimental to conversations. They're not easy to answer and they make people think too much, which essentially interrupts the flow of your conversation. If you're not supposed to ask open-ended or specific questions, what's the best course of action here?

To make any question easier to answer, put a boundary on it. A boundary lets people know exactly what you are asking, the context, and that it has a wide range of acceptable answers. That way it's not necessarily about the actual answer, but rather the discussion that follows about that topic. In a way, boundaries keep you from using absolutes in questions, which, as you saw, are difficult to answer.

For instance, "What's your favorite movie of all time?" is a tough specific question to answer, but the question, "What's a good movie you have seen recently?" is actually pretty easy. All you have to do is recall the name of a recent movie that you don't hate and the conversation can carry on. The boundaries you used to make the question easier to answer are a "good" movie that they have seen "recently." Each qualifier you use makes it easier for someone to generate an answer, and after all, someone has to do the dirty work.

So when you have a specific question, you can put boundaries and qualifiers on the question to make it less specific. It doesn't quite work the same way with broad, open-ended questions, so how can you make those types of queries work for you better?

Instead of asking an open-ended question, provide options along with the question.

"What do you like to do for fun?" becomes, "What do you like to do for fun? Do you like the outdoors, or music, or playing sports?"

Instead of asking one broad question, you've now asked one broad question and three more specific questions. See how the latter version is easier to answer because you are providing context and letting them know exactly what you want? You are also giving them a prompt in case they don't really have an answer, so they can just latch onto what you say and agree with it. Again, you are making it easy for them and allowing them to think as little as possible.

Now that we've dealt with most pointless questions you might be unknowingly asking, you can also help people and solicit better answers from them effortlessly by asking for stories instead of mere answers.

If you've ever watched sports, then you'll have seen many examples of this. Sports broadcasters interview athletes immediately after matches and games, which is probably the worst time to get a coherent thought from them because their hearts are still racing and their brains are still preoccupied from the athletic event. Nevertheless, ratings must prevail, so sportscasters ambush athletes while they are still dripping and short of breath.

It's not a time when they are very articulate, and yet sportscasters typically get decent answers from the athletes because they ask them for stories instead of mere answers or replies. Instead of asking them if they thought the match went well, they'll ask something like, "So when did you feel like the match went well? What happened to put you on the path to victory?"

See how that's a much better and meatier prompt? It elicits a story and narrative that certainly wouldn't have been the first thing out of their mouths otherwise. They are guiding the athletes and helping to form their answers for them; this is something we can do in daily life as well when we ask for stories.

Instead of asking if someone likes baseball, you could instead ask, "Have you liked baseball since you were a child? Why did you take to it over other sports?" Here, you are providing the context in your question and giving them a direction to go in that is easier for them to answer. In this case, it's actually easier to answer with a story instead of a static yes or no. And you'll be the beneficiary because this will provide exponentially more jumping off points for your conversation.

Finally, are you asking someone an oddball question or question that amounts to a conversation starter? Well, you better have an answer to it before you ask!

If you ask someone's favorite movie and they get stuck and their mind goes blank (as it often will if you ask it in a very specific way), then they'll bounce it back to you and you better have an answer or the conversation will stick right there.

Take the Hint

It's important to recognize a few verbal cues that signal that people are only interested in you to the extent that they can move on from the interaction.

If you feel that conversations seem to be drying up and going nowhere with multiple people, it's because you may be missing the signs people are sending that they either want to or need to move on.

These are so subtle you might even think they are unintentional, but in most cases, especially with people you know to be charming and conversationally fluent, it is extremely intentional.

Think of it this way—if someone is an ace baseball player, they can get on base 35 percent of the time. If you find that they are getting on base 0 percent of the time instead, it's more likely that they are doing so intentionally versus deviating that far from their natural ability.

There are three big verbal cues that will almost always signal that people are ready to disengage or that they'd like to move on sooner rather than later.

Cue of Disinterest #1: Lack of reciprocity

If you are engaging with someone and you find yourself doing most of the talking and dictating just about every part of the conversation, it's not because they just don't know what to say. It's because they are intentionally giving you one-word answers and not asking questions in the hopes that you will grow bored and move on yourself, so they don't have to do the lifting in that department. It's a mostly passive way of ending a conversation, and is the equivalent of calling in sick and then never returning to work so you don't have to handle the sticky part of leaving.

Again, it could be someone not knowing what to say, but chances are, it's an intentional precursor to a separation.

Cue of Disinterest #2: Allowing awkward silences to occur

What happens when there is an awkward silence or conversation lull?

Does the other person seem to care or make an effort? If not, they are less subtly sending you a sign that they are ready to leave. They want the awkward silence there so they can demonstrate to you that it is not an enjoyable interaction, and so they interject an excuse to leave.

Remember, if you are speaking to someone you consider charismatic or even socially adequate, it's probably uncommon for that person to have many conversation lulls and silences. If they are there, it's likely they are there intentionally and by design.

Cue of Disinterest #3: Transitioning to general topics

"So what do you have planned for the rest of the day?"

Statements like that are clear ways of signaling that someone wants to disengage. It's a not-so-subtle hint that they want to move on to the rest of *their* day.

This is especially apparent when you were on another topic, however deep and specific, and they shift gears to a general topic or future plans. It makes logical sense, actually. You can't just withdraw when you're deep within the nitty-gritty of a topic. You would feel the emotional need to see the topic to its end. However, it's much, much easier to withdraw on a general topic or what someone is going to do immediately after the conversation. It's just an easy transition to "Goodbye."

Think of it like the cool down after a workout. You can leave the gym after sprinting a mile, but you'd feel weird and unbalanced. You'd simply feel much better after cooling down and relaxing, which sets the stage for leaving.

One of the most important parts about reading people is to know when someone is no longer listening, or you are no longer welcome.

Eye Contact

People impart so much meaning and importance to people's eyes that if your eye contact is lacking, you simply fall into the pit of negative adjectives. It doesn't matter that scientific studies have consistently proven these beliefs wrong—if most people believe them, then it's true for our purposes.

What do people believe? People whole-heartedly believe that the eyes don't lie.

They believe that they can see people's character through their eyes, and a single look can determine trustworthiness and worth. It's one of the keystones of determining whether someone is lying. People use it as a North Star—their guiding light on how to read you, and what kind of person you actually are.

Thus, eye contact is quite important because it wards off negative stereotypes and attracts positive ones like confidence, power, trustworthiness, and loyalty.

But let's be clear that you don't even have to have superhuman eye contact for people to assume those traits about you. Simply having decent or passable eye contact is the bare minimum. This means that you simply can't be bad at eye contact.

When we think about the actual mechanics of great eye contact, they are simple yet supremely difficult. Why is that? Because the tension of holding eye contact is too great for you.

You're not used to it, you become alarmed and panic, and you break it. You know the feeling—it's like the other person's eyes start boring into your head.

For some of us, our tension tolerance is quite high. Personally, I feel comfortable not breaking eye contact for hours—of course, that would make me look like a maniac. But for many others, tension tolerance is a mere millisecond. That is, you start feeling tension in your eyes and have to break eye contact in less than a second.

The first step to strong eye contact is to become comfortable with it and increase the amount of eye contact tension you can tolerate. Of course, the more exposure you have to it, the more you can tolerate it.

Grab a pair of sunglasses and walk outside to an area with plenty of foot traffic. Place yourself in the path of the foot traffic, where you will be facing people walking by.

Put your sunglasses on and simply stare at people's eyes as they walk by. Remember, they can't see your eyes, so you should feel fearless in doing this.

Stare at people with impunity! You'll get exponentially more eye contact in ten minutes than you would in an entire week. Imagine how that is going to desensitize you.

Notice how even though they don't think you're looking at them, they won't make prolonged eye contact with you. Train yourself to experience the full effects of tension, all from behind the safe walls of your sunglasses. This way, you're exposing yourself fully to live eye contact but without a chance of embarrassment or rejection.

Once you feel comfortable with sunglasses, the next step is to remove them completely. Make eye contact with everyone walking by you and get used to the tension. Pretend you are playing a game called "eyes" and the winner is decided by how many seconds of eye contact he or she can achieve in the least amount of time.

Once you're able to increase your tension tolerance and hold eye contact with anyone and anything, you need to understand how to wield your new weapon wisely.

More is not always better, otherwise we would all regard television news anchors as incredibly trustworthy and loyal—

instead, the type of eye contact they use is a little unnerving and unnatural.

How much eye contact should you use?

When someone is talking to you, make eye contact 80 percent of the time.

In other words, keep their gaze and continue to look at their face while you are listening. Don't look around the room and behind them; it's distracting and gives the impression that you aren't listening. If you keep looking at them, it simply makes you look attentive and like you care what they are talking about. The 20 percent where you aren't making eye contact is important because in the same vein, staring at someone 100 percent of the time makes you appear to be zoning out and not listening. So let people feel heard and validated by maintaining eye contact with them 80 percent of the time when they are speaking.

When you are speaking to someone, make eye contact with them 50 percent of the time.

When speaking, you'll notice that it's incredibly difficult to make eye contact a majority of the time. It's because holding eye contact requires a certain percentage of your mental faculties, so when you hold eye contact, it will probably cause your train of thought to derail a bit.

But holding 100 percent eye contact when you're speaking is also a bit unnerving and makes it appear that you are lecturing or preaching to someone. Chances are that you're not a professor speaking to a class, so maintaining this kind of eye contact while speaking is highly uncomfortable for the listener.

If you've never noticed, it's downright odd to have someone staring you in the eye while speaking to you.

If you stare at someone while you speak, then you don't allow that person to react as they would naturally. You put a spotlight on them inadvertently that makes them feel pressure to react to your eye contact and words in a certain way.

Maintaining a 50 percent ratio when you speak gives the listener freedom to process your words as they please, and also allows you focus on your words instead of eye contact.

What Kind of Eye Contact Should You Use?

One of the biggest problems with eye contact is that people have the wrong perception of what constitutes good eye contact. This frequently results in what I like to call zombie eyes.

A zombie is a creature who used to be a person. That individual has died, and the zombie has risen in their place. They are undead and don't seem to have the ability for any type of meaningful thought beyond, "I'm hungry, that living creature seems pretty tasty."

Zombie eyes are dead eyes—eyes that show no emotion and no evidence of a train of thought.

This frequently happens because most people equate the amount of eye contact with its strength. In other words, the more eye contact, the better, despite the fact that in reality eye contact above a certain amount makes people supremely uncomfortable.

Zombie eyes are when someone makes eye contact with you and just stares. It's almost as if they don't even blink, they're just so intent on staring into your soul. They are expressionless and unflinching. I get uncomfortable just thinking about it.

The best way to combat zombie eyes is to contrast that facial expression with the way your eyes soften up when you are watching a video of cats wrestling and fighting. What happens?

Your eyes soften up. Your eyebrows become engaged and rise. You allow your emotions to be displayed across your face.

That's the type of eye contact you should pair with the 50 percent/80 percent ratio—that's powerful, engaging eye contact that will make you more charismatic and attractive.

Chapter 6
Always Knowing What to Say

Two of my favorite topics to cover are HPM, and more recently, SBR.

What are these strange acronyms?

Put simply, they are six distinct types of responses you can use for practically any topic that arises in a conversation. HPM and SBR are quite helpful because if you are stumped or you can see an awkward silence creeping around the corner, you can essentially use HPM and SBR as icebreaking cue cards to find topics to talk about and ways to respond to people.

It also makes sense to refer to them as a "plug and playable" because all you need to do is plug in one of these responses and bingo—it just works.

The right responses can go a long way to jump-start and add new life to your conversations. It doesn't matter how good a conversationalist you are because awkward silences are always lurking around the corner. Using HPM and SBR, you can always find a way to work around these impending conversation killers.

Here's a quick review for those of you that are new to HPM and SBR and wondering when I'm going to stop talking in annoying acronyms and codes.

HPM

HPM stands for History, Philosophy, and Metaphor.

This means in response to a question or statement directed at you, you reply with your own statement that evokes History, Philosophy, or a Metaphor.

HPM tends to draw on your memories, experiences, and opinions, which is a bit different from the other acronyms you'll be learning about in this chapter. It's more internal and personal, while others are more external and in the moment.

History means you reply with your personal experience regarding a topic. For example, if someone tells you a story about skiing, this is a prompt for you to reply with:

- That reminds me of the last time I skied . . .
- That's just like the first time I skied as a child . . .
- What a coincidence, my mother's friend went skiing last week and had a blast . . . .

Philosophy, on the other hand, involves your personal stance or opinion on a specific topic. For example, if someone tells you that same rousing story about skiing, this is a prompt for you to reply with:

- I've always loved skiing because . . .
- I've hated skiing ever since . . .
- Skiing is so fun! My favorite hobby.
- I don't know how I feel about skiing. On one hand . . .

Metaphor, on the other hand, involves what the conversation topic reminds you of. If you're hearing the same story about skiing for the third time in the same day, you might not want to talk about it again. Thus, this is a prompt for you to subtly change the topic to something that's related or . . . not so related. This works as long as you can preface it with some sort of transition.

- That reminds me of . . .
- That's just the opposite of snowboarding, isn't it?
- That makes me think of . . .
- Isn't that similar to . . .

Keep in mind that HPM is more focused on you, what you think, and what your experiences are. It really has nothing to do with the other person; it has to do with what the topic at hand evokes from you—a memory, an opinion, or feeling, or a just a general jumping-off point from which to change the subject.

Seems pretty easy and intuitive, right? The point is that everyone has these things. Everyone has personal stories and experiences, opinions, and stances on subjects, and can envision how one topic is related to or reminiscent of another topic. It's just that we are lazy conversationalists that don't realize the broad scope of what's available for us to talk about.

Here's a quick review on SBR, which you'll find is similar but probably easier to use quickly on your feet than HPM. It's external, meaning everything that you need to continue any conversational topic is right there in front of you. You'll see what I mean.

SBR

SBR stands for Specific, Broad, and Related. To any statement or question directed to you, you can reply with one of these types of statements.

Specific involves asking targeted questions regarding the topic you're talking about. This kind of response allows you to drag the conversation forward or take it deeper by pulling out fine details. Suppose you want to get into the nitty-gritty of what's being talked about. Let's take the skiing story example we used earlier:

- What kind of slopes did you go down?
- How was the snow?
- How many times have you skied recently?

Broad means you ask broad questions about the topic. These create context and are great springboards to subtopics. This enables the conversation to proceed smoothly from the main topic to a subtopic and all the way to a completely new topic. Get the background and the general lay of the land here.

- Where was this?
- Who did you go with?
- When was this?
- How did you drive there?

Finally, Related refers to asking about something that is either directly or broadly related to the subject of your conversation. The great thing about "related" is that it allows you to explore issues tangential to the topic of your conversation.

- I love when it's snowing outside.
- I love taking weekend trips.
- Isn't it great, getting physically active as much as possible?

The unifying characteristic of the SBR conversation strategy is that it focuses primarily on the topics you're talking about. That is, you're taking the exact topic that's in front of you, digging deeper into it, and essentially letting the other person guide you through questions.

So that was a fairly direct and straightforward set of rules, right? Now you have six responses you can pop into just about any situation, almost as if you're reading off of cue cards and can just say, "Oh, hmm . . . philosophy . . . well, the way I feel about that is . . ."

After a bit of brainstorming and paying attention to the fact that everyone's brain works a little bit differently, and different cues will prompt different things for people,

I developed three more frameworks that are usable in just about any situation: EDR.

Using these nine frameworks together adds a whole lot of engagement, personalization, depth, and intrigue to a conversation that might otherwise have begun and ended at "Hey, how was your weekend?"

EDR

EDR is the last part of the nine frameworks that you can use to answer just about anything. It straddles HPM and SBR—you can use what's in front of you, but it's even better if you draw internally and speak about your own thoughts and opinions.

EDR stands for Emotion, Detail, and Restatements.

E (emotion) means when you respond to a statement made in conversation, you state someone else's emotion or emotional state.

You mention what you believe their emotional response will be. For example, "It seems like you're really excited about that." If it's not 100 percent apparent and clear to you what the other person's emotional state is, you can make a statement summing up an assumption to see whether you're right or not. You don't have to be correct, the point is that whether you are or not, they will correct you and automatically explain their actual feelings.

"I went skiing last weekend!"

"You sound really excited about that."

If you were wrong: "Actually, I'm not. Here's why . . ."

If you were right: "Totally, it was very thrilling to be on the slopes."

Think of this like being a very open-minded counselor who just wants to talk about other people's feelings. When you state someone's emotions, you appear to be very in tune with them and engaged in their well-being.

To emphasize, what makes this approach particularly effective is that you talk about other people's emotions, not yours.

As I've mentioned in my previous books, people like to be the center of attention. The more attention you give them, the more they're likely to talk. In "E," you allow them to take the limelight and express their emotions. People appreciate this because most people like to feel they matter, and they aren't often given a chance to feel that way.

"D" (detail) means when you respond to a topic, you do so by asking for details and how they relate to the person with whom you're speaking. This is similar to the "S" in SBR.

You get the details and you also get an overview of how it impacts them. For example, the key journalistic "5 Ws" work perfectly here. The 5 Ws, just in case you don't know, are who, what, where, when, and why. The 5 Ws work perfectly because they allow you to tie in different details to the person with whom you're speaking. Think of yourself as a detective sifting through different clues to solve a mystery.

For example, the questions, "When did you start doing that?" or "How did that make you feel?" and so on. These interrogatives help you get a direct answer.

"R" (restatements) means when you respond to a topic, you do so by restating or summarizing what the other person said and then throw it back at them.

This is very effective because it lets the person you're speaking with know that you're paying attention to them. You're paying so much attention that you can't get their words out of your mouth!

As I mentioned above, people like to feel they matter. What better way to show that appreciation than simply letting them know, in clear terms, that you were listening to what they had to say and you want confirmation of your understanding of what they've said?

When you restate what they say, you are essentially validating them twice. First, the simple act of summarizing what they said already validates them. It lets them know that you were listening to them. On top of that, you ask for their permission or confirmation to see if you've understood them correctly. This creates a tremendous sense of comfort and validation for the other person.

"I went skiing in the mountains last weekend."

"So you went skiing in the *mountains* last weekend?"

"So you went *skiing* in the mountains last weekend?"

"So you went skiing in the mountains *last weekend*?"

This prompts them to elaborate on their statement without your having to say much. All you did was say the exact same thing back to them, with a slight emphasis on a different word to indicate that you are curious and want clarification on an aspect of what they've said. Each of these three versions is a distinctly different assertion or question, but you are using their exact words.

Think of this like a psychologist prompting a patient for deeper and more personal discoveries and insights.

By using EDR in addition to HMP and SBR, you now have nine ways to respond to people about anything.

Which of the nine feel easy and natural to you and which feel difficult?

Pay careful attention, because as previously noted, some of these are more about your own thoughts and internal workings, and others are about the situation in front of you and the other person. So if you skew too much in one direction, it can mean you're either a conversational narcissist or someone who provides no value or substance.

Chain them together and with these nine techniques you will pretty much never run out of things to talk about.

Provide More Information

If you feel your conversations are lacking spice and intrigue, it's probably because you are speaking without saying much at all.

People find that they subconsciously expect others to let their guards down without any reason. You need to provide more personal information, opinions, and specific details when you speak to people. It's as simple as that. It's one thing to never run out of things to say, but it's another thing to actually say things that people care about.

This is a tough step for many because it's a muscle they aren't used to flexing. They aren't used to talking about themselves at any length, and when they are asked about their weekends, they tend to say it was just "good." Does this describe you?

You can't just depend on others to draw it out of you or for them to share first. When you give general responses, you'll get general answers. When you broach general subjects, you'll remain on shallow, surface-level topics. And when you stay general and not personal, all you'll eventually gain are acquaintances and not necessarily friends. You need to share unsolicited information—because that's what friends do.

Think back to the last engaging, entertaining conversation you had with a friend. What was the topic, and what was said about it? You might not remember the topic, but you remember that you felt comfortable and unfiltered when discussing it. This is the type of tone you want to use with everyone because when you treat someone like a stranger, they will act like a stranger.

You don't need permission to speak like a friend or treat someone with familiarity. The vast majority of what you think is too forward or inappropriate actually is not. Imagine a friend broaching that topic of stance, and then you'll see that it's completely acceptable.

You also need to share more details about yourself, which allows people to relate better and to find shared interests and commonalities. Do people know a lot about you, or are you generally regarded as an enigma to them? Don't discount the value of being more relatable to others; it will make you more likable on many levels.

We instinctively hunt for similarities and shared interests whenever we meet someone, so help them find it by revealing more personal details. If you answer someone that your weekend was "good, but tiring," you are doing yourself a disservice if you could instead say your weekend was "good.

I went skiing in the mountains and it was really tiring." You might find that they also love skiing.

The significance of finding similarities with people is huge. If you were born in a small town of five hundred people, and you randomly meet someone from the same town in bustling New York City, you would be drawn to them immediately. You'd be thrilled to meet them because you would see them as similar in worldview, understanding, and values. Familiarity is comforting and attractive.

Beyond sharing personal information, the other major facet of your personality to share more of is your opinion. It's understandable that many are reticent to do so for various reasons, such as judgment, people-pleasing tendencies, or discomfort with confrontation, but opinion-sharing doesn't necessarily need to lead to any of those things. As you can see, the theme of this chapter isn't necessarily that you need to know more to always know what to say—the knowledge and statements that you should share are usually already within you. We have opinions, personal details, and even emotions, but we don't outright state or express them as we can and should.

Sharing an opinion on a topic is simply saying something with substance, as opposed to, "Well, you know, it was tough, but it was fair. Both sides are right and also wrong. It could go either way." It's the equivalent of asking someone what they want to eat for dinner and then having them hesitate and hedge endlessly. The actual restaurant isn't important, but people typically get upset at the lack of an opinion.

You don't have to express your opinions militantly and without regret. There are certainly ways of making a stance known.

The easiest way to share more is to actually form your opinions, no matter how slight or uninformed. You just have something to say instead of saying, "I don't know, what do you think?"

You can do this before interactions to make sure you aren't someone who speaks but says nothing. This is similar to the Conversation Resume, where you should find the biggest topics are in the following categories:

- Current events
- Pop culture
- Interpersonal situations amongst your friends
- Your preferences and pet peeves
- Hypothetical situations you are likely to run into

Form a tentative opinion on them, and review them so you will have something to say about these topics. It's similar to the classic quandary of asking a friend where they want to eat dinner. They can either express an opinion, or they can keep punting back to you, insisting that they don't care. They might think they are being easy-going and low-maintenance, but in fact it puts more of the burden on the other person who is given nothing to work with.

You're not wedded to your opinion once you make it or state it. It's just your opinion based on the information you have, and you should maintain the mindset that you are open to discussion and correction if need be. As long as you don't state them with an air of knowledge or the attitude that you know better, an opinion by itself will never expose you to judgment. Instead, it's how you react to an opinion's acceptance of rejection that will expose you to judgment.

If you are unable to construct opinions, it means you need to consume more information to educate yourself better. Personal details and opinions are something we can always share more of to fill the air.

The Only Two Storytelling Methods You Need

The final aspect of always knowing what to say is storytelling. I tend to get a lot of questions about storytelling.

In reality, it's one of the things that I try to simplify as much as possible in my answers. There are many ways you can approach it. You can approach it in the sense that you're a standup comedian and you want to captivate people, or as if you're around a campfire and trying to draw people in.

You can also even take inspiration from the literary cliché of the hero's journey, which demonstrates how structured stories can be.

For daily conversation, though, I'm not a fan of storytelling. Why not?

Primarily, because chances are you're not a professional storyteller or standup comedian. None of us can think on that level in the course of daily conversation—not while we're trying to keep up with others and react to them in real time. So for storytelling, I like to keep it simple with two main methods that clients have reported the most success with. These two methods also tie into my previous point about sharing more personal information and details.

Remember, many people have enough trouble listening to others, so it's a tall task to ask them to keep an outline in their heads. So forget the three-part hero's journey and just focus on keeping people's attention for a small amount of time, then on the discussion afterwards. After all, you aren't a movie. So let's simplify storytelling and make sure people don't wander off far before you get to your climax or punch line.

Storytelling Method #1: Just give five distinct, specific details and forget building a narrative

This is as simple as it gets. You only need to be able to count to five.

Have a story about your weekend that involves skiing? Great, then give five distinct, specific details about your weekend, and you'll find that you'll get better reactions than ever before.

Why does this work? Four details are often insufficient to establish a narrative, while six details verges into over-sharing and conversational monopolization territory. Five details is the perfect balance, and saying them out loud allows you to find your narrative as you're saying it.

Finally, you must make sure to give *specific* details because they are what give your story life and make it relatable.

For example, here are five vague details: I went skiing with someone, had a tough time, but it was fun, and I'm now very tan.

Here are five specific details: I went skiing with my older brother, almost broke my leg, loved it because I hadn't seen him for over a year, and got incredibly sunburned from the snow reflection. I also had the best steak I've ever had in my life at the ski lodge.

See the difference? The specific details can lead to separate topics all by themselves. Specific details are *not* mere names, locations, or additional facts about the weather. Every piece of information should lead to a different piece of information, so your story now becomes five topics someone can hook onto if they wish. The details don't have to be about the same thing, event, or person. They're just five details you are giving another person so they can find something of interest that they might want to ask about. In essence, you are making it as easy for them as possible.

So employ the KISS method: keep it simple, stupid. Just give five distinct details. It will keep you from talking people's ears off, and also make sure that you aren't speaking without saying anything. Storytelling doesn't have to be in the style of Homer.

Storytelling Method #2: Focus on one emotion in one sentence

At the heart of it, we tell stories to evoke an emotional reaction of some sort in the other person. Though there are somewhere between five to seven primary emotions, as science says, there are only so few primary emotions we are actually seeking when we share a story with someone.

Usually, those emotions are some variation of happiness, commiseration, shock, or interest. You can classify those reactions under whatever emotion you wish. What's important is that you know what you are trying to convey.

If you want to tell a story about getting cut off in traffic, you probably want to convey shock and commiseration. You want them to proclaim, "What a horrible person!" with you.

With that in mind, attempt to tell your story in one sentence at first. The purpose of this is to battle droning on while you try to find the point out loud. If you can summarize your story in one sentence, it means you actually know what it's about and what the important parts are.

Having this type of focus on something as simple as a story can make a huge difference in how you present it. Can you summarize a psychological theory—or even a movie—in one sentence? If you can, it shows understanding of the important parts and what you can omit without consequence.

If you feel the need to explain Disney's *Aladdin* in three sentences, it probably means you don't remember it very well and have no recollection of some major plot points. The more succinctly you can state something, the better you understand it—this is the version of your story that your friends want to hear. They don't want to hear your unorganized mess.

For example, if I want to tell the same story about my weekend, what do I want to convey? Generally, I want to show how fun it was and the happiness it gave me.

Then, how can you condense your weekend into one sentence? By focusing on the events that further the sentiment of fun and happiness. For instance, "We went skiing and it was really fun because . . ."

It's worth noting that both of these storytelling methods make you a much briefer and clearer storyteller. This is an optimal trait because stories are about conveying a point and emotion, not captivating people. People want to interact with you and have a two-way dialogue, not listen to you like you're a professor. If you want to captivate an audience, step onto a stage!

Chapter 7
Breaking into Banter

One of the biggest questions I get on a regular basis regards how to break out of small talk interview mode and into something that actually resembles how real friends talk.

The question is essentially how to transition from talking about something serious to nothing at all, because this is actually the progression of the vast majority of interactions we have with our friends. We might be discussing the latest current events in a comfortable manner, but the feeling people are really after when they want to break out of small talk interview mode is the feeling of being able to joke around and just banter with someone.

What do you talk to your friends about? You probably can't remember the last few topics unless they happened to make you extremely happy or extremely sad. What happens when we spend time with our friends is we just enjoy their company and take pleasure in the type of interaction we receive from them. You remember the emotion and that you had a good time, but you don't remember the topic of conversation because it just isn't important.

Take the television show *Seinfeld*, for instance. For years detractors derided it as a "show about nothing," where the characters did nothing, and the majority of the show really took place in either a café or the apartment of the titular character, Jerry Seinfeld.

The topics weren't inherently engaging or grabbing, but you'll find the comedy lauded in almost every top ten of any list of television comedies you'll ever read. This is because people just felt like they were watching friends interact, banter, and joke around. That's the feeling we want, and it's important to realize that it's about the *tone and dynamic* of the conversation, not necessarily the topic.

A common theme on *Seinfeld* was taking a small issue, blowing it out of proportion, and then watching the various sets of reactions to it unfold. For instance, there is a famous episode where one of the main characters, George, states that he cannot date a woman because of the peculiar way one of her toes looks.

There are a few tones and dynamics you can take to a topic like this.

Jerry Seinfeld could take a severe and serious tone, as if he were lambasting George's shallowness and lack of priorities. Elaine, the main female character, could try to talk to George about his self-destructive tendencies and how he self-sabotages his most promising relationships because of his terrible relationship with his mother. The wildcard character,

Kramer, would invite George out to play golf to take his mind off things and delay judgment to a later time in the future.

You could go any of those routes.

But you could also adopt the tone and dynamic of joking around with the topic, making fun of it, debating it hypothetically, and trying to draw outlandish conclusions as to why a toe issue might bother someone so much.

That's the route the writers of that episode took, and it is illustrative of the fact that it's not the topic that matters, but how you approach it.

There are two ways to speak, generally.

First, when you speak to someone like a friend, you aren't afraid of judgment and you freely speak your mind. You aren't worried about filtering yourself so someone will accept you, and you are generally *yourself*.

Second, when you speak to someone like an acquaintance or stranger, you hold that person at arm's length and stay formal. You are filtering yourself and your thoughts because your highest priority is to not offend.

So, which do you use more frequently? It seems obvious when you create two categories that you should speak to everyone you meet like a friend because it puts them at ease and encourages rapport. If you speak to a person any other way, then you are setting the tone and giving the implication that you **want** to be formal and at arm's length. Speak familiarly, be familiar.

Playing vs. Discussing

This can also be called "Amusing vs. Conversing." There are many ways to look at these two different modes of thought.

The default conversation approach most people use is, of course, to discuss and converse. There's nothing wrong with that, and it can certainly lead to interesting revelations. However, it's exclusively what strangers and co-workers do. When you seek to make deeper connections and build rapport as friends, there may be elements of discussing involved, but there are far more elements of playing.

It's not the ideal way to build rapport since it can be a dry discussion of facts and news, which doesn't tell you anything about a person's personality, nor does it allow you to show your own off. People discuss current events with colleagues. People play with and amuse friends with personal stories. See the difference?

The difference in mindset should be to focus on being more playful, as exemplified in a *Seinfeld* episode, not taking people at face value, and not worrying about answering questions literally. Just because they asked about the weather doesn't mean that you are only allowed to talk about the weather.

Actively think about how you react to someone in a playful manner. Imagine how you would react if you were five years old, and that is honestly a better approximation for playful conversation that can build rapport. If someone asks you about the weather, what are the different ways you can reply?

You can ask silly questions, you can say things solely to see how others respond. You might create outlandish hypotheticals, you can address the elephant in the room, you can allow your inner monologue to be read out loud, and so on. When you're playing, you are satisfying the main goals of conversation we've laid out multiple times—entertainment and allowing another person to be lazy—while also amusing yourself.

You may generally view the other person as someone to joke around with, as opposed to someone to make a professional first impression on. You can even view them as a backdrop to entertain yourself with. You don't need to give people straight, exact answers. People are usually far more attracted to interesting and noteworthy answers. Unless you are giving an oral report, it's not a stretch to say that they would always prefer something to catch their attention versus be dry and accurate.

Remember that you're not necessarily looking to absorb a set of facts, or extract certain information. Instead, your goal is simply to feel good around those people and, most importantly, make them feel good around you.

Word of caution: you can be both humorous and informative. Make sure to occasionally check in with the other person to make sure that you aren't going overboard with the lack of substantive content if they're seeking it.

Think Non-Linear

Usually, we imagine conversations to be structured in a very linear manner.

You start with Point A, you proceed to go through the agenda of Point A and its subtopics, then you begin with Point B, and so on down the list. That works perfectly if you're in a boardroom going over a corporate agenda.

If you're trying to build rapport and have an enjoyable interaction, it pays off tremendously to think in non-linear terms. This means acknowledging Point A, while moving to

Point B, then going straight to Point D, and looping back to Point A only at the end of the conversation.

That's the real winding path of a conversation. Relaxed, organic conversations are not very predictable, so you need to be able to adapt. Don't feel the need to stay on one topic, a related topic, or even an appropriate topic.

It is completely acceptable to transition from the weather to cars, to types of bread, to shopping for jeans. There doesn't have to be a transition between any two topics, and there doesn't need to be any transition when you want to bring back an older topic. That's a major sticking point some people have, simply because they feel like it might be awkward to suddenly bring up a new topic. But, is it awkward when you do it with your friends? It isn't, which means that this is an assumption based on social fear.

Make your conversation non-linear by simply talking about what you want. If you think about it this way, there is no way you can feel trapped in a topic. You are only trapped because you let yourself be.

By thinking about your conversation in non-linear terms, you take away a lot of its tendency to be dull, boring, and "heavy." You can lighten things up by jumping from topic to subtopic and then back to the main topic again. You can keep yourself entertained, and make sure to keep others amused and engaged as well. This increases the likelihood that the other person would also be in an adventurous and playful mood.

In a roundabout manner, this means you shouldn't be going into conversations with agendas and overarching goals. If you stick to those agendas, you'll be trying to force conversations into linear thinking, and feel hopelessly lost when you deviate from that agenda. The only goal you might want to focus on is to treat them in a familiar way and create entertainment.

What Would Sebastian Do?

If you want to be funny, it's a good idea to study people who make their living being funny. Professional comedians can teach you volumes about delivery and finding openings and opportunities. You also get a tremendous array of potential humor role models.

As of the time of writing this book, Sebastian Maniscalco is my favorite comedian.

He's funny, but he also has well-defined personality traits. He views the trappings of modern life from his immigrant father who tries to cut a deal at unlikely places such as the dentist. He's cranky, critical, observant, petty, easily annoyed, grumpy, and easily indignant. Having that list of adjectives makes it pretty easy for me to simply ask, "What would Sebastian do in this situation?" or, "How might Sebastian respond here?"

You can start looking at situations based on the comedian's perspective. By simply assuming their perspective, you're more able to find the humor in certain topics that you used to think were so serious. You're able to step out of your mindset and into someone else's.

Humor is a point of view, and you are using another person's.

Suppose it is Halloween night, and you are wearing a vampire costume. It's pretty easy to imagine how you might play that role, right? Having a comedic role model does the same for you, and makes it easy when you run out of things to say, or your mind blanks.

You can step into their shoes and look at situations in a novel way, and at the very least, you can find more options in how to approach humorous situations. If I can imagine what Sebastian would say, then I won't have a blank mind or run out of things to say.

Think Slightly Inappropriate

This is a mindset that you should act carefully on, and only when you are sure of yourself.

It's predicated on the fact that when you talk about "appropriate topics," they usually turn out to be boring and shallow. There are only so many interesting things you can say about work, the weather, grocery shopping, or ice skating. We stay on these topics because we feel like anything more and we are invading people's privacy and secrets. It's not true, but it's a mental barrier we place on ourselves to err on the side of caution, not realizing that the window of appropriateness continues to shrink.

That means in order to have better, funnier conversations, you need to skew towards the slightly inappropriate.

What do you speak about to your close friends? I'd bet you don't stick to appropriate and professional topics. Inappropriateness gets people talking and laughing, and almost no one is ever offended by it. There is a limit you may have put on yourself to keep things appropriate, and that unfortunately keeps you conversationally vanilla, and your relationships remain cold and distant because people don't think they can open up to you beyond a certain level.

You can do this in two ways.

The first way is to have a slightly inappropriate take on a boring topic: "Ice skating? I just saw this YouTube clip where someone's ear was sliced off from a skate!"

The second way is to bring up a slightly inappropriate topic by itself: "Yeah, ice skating is fun. I think I only like figure skating because of the crazy costumes the competitors wear."

When you introduce something slightly inappropriate (slightly being subjective), you put others at ease.

When you get people laughing and relaxed around you, this gives you the opening to establish rapport. When you break the boredom with inappropriateness, you're doing them a favor by going beyond the conventional and predictable. This is going to feel uncomfortable and difficult at first, and might even be one of the most difficult tips in this book to master. But all you have to do is remember two things: You talk to your friends in one way and acquaintances in another, so it's your choice as to how to treat people. Second, if you filter yourself endlessly around people, and you succeed in making them like you, then whom do they actually like?

Intentionally Misconstrue

Another prime method of breaking into banter is to misconstrue what people say, but intentionally. You're looking for opportunities for light misunderstanding, double entendre, puns, and comical confusion.

Usually, people try to police these and make sure they understand the other person as clearly as possible. If you are trying to speak to a friend, you don't take what they say at face value. In many cases, you're actively trying to undermine what they say by deliberately misunderstanding them so you can make fun of them or make light of a situation.

Some of the funniest situations I've seen in both movies and real life have come from simple misunderstandings.

For example, Bob misunderstood what a proctologist did and scheduled four appointments, or Jenny misunderstood that the generic name for a painkiller is an analgesic, and is not pronounced nor administered the way she thought it was. Which one of those was from real life and which was from a movie? Well, both were from real life.

Those are instances of lightning caught in a bottle. Wouldn't it be great to create those moments when you want? You can take the lead instead of waiting for an opportunity to arise and essentially relying upon luck.

Misunderstanding and misinterpretation are great sources of humor because you play with two sets of expectations and operate in the gray area between them.

Sometimes you have to be intentional about setting these misunderstandings yourself, and that is the Art of Misconstruing: misunderstanding people in an intentional manner to bring about a comical situation.

In other words, playing dumb or confused and taking an entirely different meaning from what someone has said on purpose. It's one of the easiest and quickest ways to bring the conversation to a playful nature and break the mold of small talk conversation.

Think of it as a transition from a boring topic into a more engaging conversation. Whatever perspective you take, it's simply a shift toward both parties enjoying themselves more.

The misconstruing tactic requires you to stay in character for a split second while you do it. Strangely and counter-intuitively, this requires people to think for a split second that you truly mean what you say. Otherwise, you convey mixed messages, and your words don't match up with the rest of your non-verbal or verbal delivery.

After that split second has passed, it will become obvious through your words and your delivery that you are obviously making a joke.

Here's a simplified example of misconstruing: when someone says, "I like cats," you might reply with, "To eat?" Pair your words with a shocked look on your face and eyes wide open. That's the character you are trying to convey.

You've misconstrued the other person by not picking up on their context or intent. Imagine how a foreigner might interpret those words because of a weak grasp of the English language. Where does the conversation go from there?

They'll likely join the banter with you and agree, such as, "Yeah, but only stray cats. The domesticated ones are too fat."

Misconstruing is one of the most common ways of creating a humorous situation. It is the basis of many jokes because it's easy to take a situation and steer it in whatever direction you want. It allows you to initiate a joke with people in most situations.

It also helps you break out of typical, boring topics. By simply choosing to misconstrue, you can inject whatever perspective you want into a conversation at any point.

It's freeing and empowering! It doesn't get old and it can go a long way in adding life to an otherwise generic or boring conversation.

What are some ways to misconstrue in a funny way?

Exaggerated Conclusion

This is where you misconstrue what someone says and take it to the extreme conclusion.

You exaggerate what they say to an exponential degree. If someone actually said X, you would pretend that they said X multiplied by one hundred and react accordingly.

For example, when someone says, "I love my television," you might reply, "So do your parents know that you guys are living together before marriage?"

Instead of saying "I agree," or coming up with a statement on the same vein or at the same intensity as the original statement, take the original statement and blow it out of proportion and to a different context.

If somebody says a politician has a good point, a really funny exaggeration would be, "Yes, he is the epitome of this country's political evolution, let's use him for breeding."

It is all about blowing up somebody's statement to an absurd and exaggerated form.

Another example: "That coffee was terrible!" You could reply, "I agree, my car's battery water is tastier."

What makes this form of misconstruing powerful is the absurdity of your exaggeration. It should be so absurd that it is no longer believable. That's where the humor comes from. A lot of people screw up this technique when they don't exaggerate enough.

They fall somewhere in between the truly funny exaggerated form and the generic statement. If you want to use this technique, make sure you really blow it up and make it out of this world. That way it's obvious to the other person that you are making fun and they can laugh along.

Sarcasm

Sarcasm is a way for people to say things without saying them. Think about how Chandler Bing from the television show, *Friends*, speaks. If he says something is wonderful, he says *it's wonnnnderful* in a tone that immediately lets you know that he thinks the opposite.

Sarcasm functions like a social cue: a way to express something without having to explicitly say it. In that way, it's a great device for handling uncomfortable topics or pointing out the elephant in the room without directly offending people (or actually pointing). It allows us to walk a tightrope, as long as we don't fall into the pit of passive-aggressiveness.

At some level, most of us can appreciate sarcasm because we know what is being accomplished. It can even be the basis for your own personal brand of humor. Standup comics often use it to great effect.

Chances are you are already using it regularly without being fully aware of it.

This chapter is about arming you with the exact elements of most sarcasm that you can use expertly for better conversations, banter, and humor. Sarcasm is mostly used as friendly banter with a friend or acquaintance you are comfortable saying something negative around.

Sarcasm is usually used to poke fun at someone or something, and is heavily context- and audience-dependent. If you are around somebody who enjoys wit and has a sarcastic sense of humor, it will be quite welcome.

But around others who don't share the same sense of humor, are less secure, or simply don't like you, it's too easy for them to interpret your attempts at sarcastic humor as a full-fledged insult. That's not what you're aiming for here.

Using it in the wrong context will cause people to think you lack empathy or, worse, get your jollies from hurting other people's feelings.

However, choose the correct context and sarcasm can make you more likeable and charming. It also makes you look intelligent and witty. In some social circles, appropriate levels of sarcasm are not only welcomed, but required.

Now that you have a clearer idea about the proper context of sarcasm, the next step is to articulate the elements to make sure you don't just insult people left and right in your attempts at building rapport. If your annoying coworker understood sarcasm better, they might be as funny as they think they are.

For the most part, sarcasm is saying the *opposite* of (1) an objective fact, (2) a subjective emotion, or (3) a thought.

It makes a contradictory statement about a situation to either emphasize or downplay its effect.

Objective fact: Bob plays Tetris at work constantly.

Sarcastic statement: *Bob, you are the busiest man I know.*

Subjective emotion or thought: It is hilarious that Bob plays Tetris at work constantly.

Sarcastic statement: *Bob deserves a medal for worker of the year.*

Here's another one.

Objective fact: There is a surprising amount of traffic lately.

Sarcastic statement: *What are we going to do when we get to our destination super early?*

Subjective emotion or thought: I hate traffic so much.

Sarcastic statement: *This traffic is the best part of my day.*

That's the first and most common use of sarcasm. Let's lay out a framework for different types of sarcasm and exactly when and how you can use it. You'll be surprised how formulaic and methodical you can get with this, and subsequently with humor.

When someone says something or does something very obvious, you respond by saying something equally obvious.

Bob: "That road is very long."
You: "You are very observant."

Bob: "It's so hot today!"
You: "I see you're a meteorologist in training."

Poor Bob: "This menu is huge!"
You: "Glad to see you've learned to read!"

The next application of sarcasm is when something good or bad happens. You say something about how that event reflects on the other person.

If it's good, you say that it reflects poorly on them; if it's bad, you say it reflects well on them.

Bob: "I dropped my coffee mug."
You: "You've always been so graceful."

Bob: "I got an F on my math test."
You: "Now I know who to call when my calculator breaks."

You observe Poor Bob dropping a cup of coffee and state, "You would make a great baseball catcher. Great hands!"

Proper delivery is crucial for sarcasm. This can mean the difference between people laughing at your sarcastic joke, or thinking that you're serious in your sentiment and an overall jerk.

You have to make it clear that you're being sarcastic and give them a sign indicating your sarcasm. Otherwise, people will feel uncomfortable at the uncertainty. Are you just being mean, or are you trying to be funny?

The most common way to do this is with a combination of a deadpan vocal tone and a wry smile or smirk. With deadpan delivery, you don't laugh while you're saying it; you appear completely serious. Then, you break into a smile to alleviate the tension and clue them in to your true intention.

Now that you know when to deliver sarcastic remarks, it's also important to learn about how to receive them and be a good audience. Let's pretend that you are Poor Bob from earlier, and insert a reply for him.

Bob: "That road is very long."
You: "You are very observant."
Redeemed Bob: "You know it. I'm like an eagle."

Bob: "It's so hot today!"
You: "I see you're a meteorologist in training."
Redeemed Bob: "I can feel it in my bones. It's my destiny."

Poor Bob: "This menu is huge!"
You: "Glad to see you've learned to read!"
Redeemed Bob: "I can also count to ten."

You need to amplify their statement and what they are implying. Does this look familiar? It's a self-deprecating remark, plus a witty comeback!

When you respond to sarcasm this way, it creates a greater bond. Everybody is comfortable, and you create a funny situation and potential for greater banter.

And just as important, you don't come off as a bad sport or someone who can't take a joke.

A lot of people who rely on sarcastic humor, pretty much on an automatic basis, are actually masking passive-aggressive personalities. They're constantly using sarcasm as a defense mechanism to hide their true feelings and to pass off their otherwise negative emotions. They might be doing this to you, so it's important to know how to sidestep their subconsciously vicious attacks.

Sarcasm? It's *soooooo lame,* isn't it?

The Witty Comeback Machine

The final way of breaking into banter is to become skilled at witty comebacks.

As a former fat kid, I used to have a fairly extensive library of witty comebacks for those charming people who liked to point out that I was, indeed, still as fat as I was the day before.

Or that they couldn't ride in a car with me for fear of it tipping over. Or that I was so big my Polo brand sport shirt had a *real* horse on it (this one was pretty clever, I'll admit).

Mind you, I wasn't really that large—just twenty pounds overweight. At some point, however, I developed one type of comeback that never failed to either shut people up, or bring them to my side through laughter.

112

Were you aware that my Polo Sport shirt can also be used as a parachute?

You better put two extra wheels on your car for me!

What exactly are these lines composed of, and why are they so effective?

Becoming a witty comeback machine is easier than you think, and it's one of the best conversational tactics you can learn. It doesn't only rear its head when dealing with insults—it is widely applicable once you learn the framework. If it's a bad situation, a witty comeback can diffuse the tension and bring emotional levels back to normal. If it's a good situation, then a witty comeback can make it even better.

Whatever the situation, mastering witty comebacks will earn you the respect of other people for your clever wit. It just takes one line—and the shorter and punchier, the better and more effective.

A witty comeback does many things simultaneously. It makes people laugh and disarms them, while allowing you to appear smart, insightful, and mentally quick.

But before I get ahead of myself, let me define what a witty comeback is. Wit is essentially spontaneous creativity. You take a topic or statement and see it from a different angle in a way that is relatable, yet novel. That's why I kind of enjoyed the aforementioned joke about the Polo Sport shirt, even if it was at my expense.

Witty comebacks can be hurtful, serious, or completely light and harmless. It all depends on you. You can be joking and playing around, or you can wield a sharp sword.

For the purposes of this book, you want to use wit to disarm people. So it's the former you should aim for, lest you create major tension. There's a fine line between destructive and teasing.

What's tricky about wit is that something that may be funny and completely harmless to you can be destructive or hurtful to someone else. You have to know where that fine line is and you have to know how to straddle it.

There are a few tricks to always having a witty comeback in your pocket ready for launch instead of twenty minutes after the encounter.

First, when thinking about a witty comeback, don't think generically.

Don't use the clichés, "I know you are, but what am I?" or, "So is your mom." People judge a witty comeback based on how original it is—remember, it's spontaneous creativity. Using something that is both generic and banal is decidedly neither spontaneous nor creative. Don't just use a template-driven witty comeback that you've seen in a movie or something that better works in a totally unrelated context. And don't use one of the comebacks you thought were hilarious when you were ten. Those don't work anymore.

Second, don't act like you can't take a joke.

Of course, witty comebacks need an initial statement to "come back" to.

The vast majority of the time, people are indeed joking when they say something negative about you in your presence. In a sense, it's a compliment because they assume you have a sufficient sense of humor and the emotional resiliency to deal with it. The people who aren't involved in jokes and good-natured ribbing don't have many friends.

If you let it show that you are angry or hurt, it spoils the playful tone you could otherwise enhance with your witty comeback.

For example, if someone made a joke about my fatness, and I got visibly angry, they would likely stop . . . then walk on eggshells around me for days. When someone is uncomfortable with something, they make others uncomfortable as well. If that happens enough times, then it becomes clear that I don't have a sense of humor and I let my insecurity infect my relationships.

Handle the initial negative statement with a wry smirk and with the knowledge that you are about to crush them.

Third, use the right tone.

The best witty comebacks are delivered with 50 percent indifference. When you deliver one with 100 percent excitement and 0 percent indifference, guess what happens? You blow it and the comeback falls flat. Indifference is the correct tone because comebacks are about your attitude—pretend that you are James Bond delivering a witty retort after a failed murder attempt by a villain. Fifty percent indifference also ensures that you aren't being aggressive or hateful.

A witty comeback is the verbal equivalent of Judo or Aikido—using an opponent's words against them. If you take that analogy, you need a certain amount of cool to effectively counteract. Witty comebacks take the power away from the insult hurled.

There are four main types of witty comebacks.

None are better than the other. You just need to pick the type you're most comfortable with.

Type #1: Pick Apart Their Words

Think about the other person's word choice and quickly analyze whether there is another angle or meaning to those words. An easy approach is to interpret their words as overly literal or outlandish. The key is to interpret them in a way that is favorable to you to make it seem as if they complimented you instead of put you down.

> Bob: *You are working as slow as a glacier. Pick it up!*
>
> You: [focusing on the word glacier] *You mean I'm super strong and cool under pressure? True.*

Type #2: Agree and Amplify

The idea here is to agree with whatever the insult was, and then add to it in an absurd way. You amplify the initial sentiment to a degree that is ridiculous. This was my go-to technique to deflect jokes about my weight.

For example:

> Bob: *Your cooking was pretty terrible last time.*
>
> You: *You're lucky you didn't stay until the end of the night, we all got our stomachs pumped.*

Type #3: Reverse and Amplify

This is a simple deflection. This is when you get back at them in a subtle way. When someone says you are bad at X, you basically turn it around by saying that they are even worse at X.

It's the exact same as the previous type of witty comeback, except instead of directing the amplification at yourself, you direct it to the other person.

Bob: *Your cooking was pretty terrible last time.*

You: *Yeah, but at least I didn't need to get my stomach pumped the way I did after the last time you cooked!*

Type #4: Use an Outlandish Comparison

This brings the conversation into a different sphere and makes both people laugh at the weird outlandish imagery. What makes this work is that the comparison, although extreme, is still somewhat realistic. To use the same framework, you're amplifying (to yourself or the other person) with an analogy here.

Bob: *Your cooking was pretty terrible last time.*

You: *True, I should have used the eggs as hockey pucks, right?*

Witty comebacks are the blood of witty banter, which is being able to take an element of what was said and attack it from a different angle without missing a beat. You should be able to see how this can play out. They are instant retorts that aren't hostile or combative, while addressing something gracefully. What more can you ask for?

Word of caution: fight the temptation to rattle comebacks off one after the other. Again, you have to remember that your goal is to get people to like you. You're not trying to prove a point or protect your pride.

You're just trying to keep your conversation from hitting awkward spots and dying a premature death. Firing off one comeback after another can kill whatever level of comfort you've managed to create because you will appear insecure, defensive, and full of bluster.

Chapter 8
Creating Flow

Without fail, I've found that one of the most effective ways to simplify and think about conversation is to liken it to an improv comedy performance. It's an important comparison to make because everyone wants a conversation that flows, adapts, and seems to have no sense of lulls or silences. That's exactly the goal of improv comedy. It's almost too perfect when you really look at them side by side.

Let's spell out the similarities.

Both a conversation and an improv comedy performance involve parties who can't read each other's minds. They are both unpredictable situations because you just never know what is going to come out of someone's mouth.

Both situations have the same goal of creating a pleasurable interaction; the conversation is enjoyable for the participants, and the improv comedy performance for the audience.

Both situations require collaboration and listening to create a dialogue, otherwise it's just two people reciting monologues to each other, or speaking over each other.

Finally, both situations are *fragile*. As you well know from your own experience, the wrong word, phrase, or question can instantly send a conversation into the toilet, and it's the same for an improv comedy performance. One miscue or misread from the other performer, and a silence will consume the stage, leading the audience to realize that this was indeed an unplanned stumble.

If you've ever attended an improv comedy show, you'll know that the performers often refer to themselves as players, just like teammates on a sports team. This is not insignificant: it instantly frames what you see on stage as a collaborative effort where everyone is supporting everyone else for the common good.

If any of the players sense that someone needs support, they will instantly give it. They understand that the performance isn't about any one person in particular—it's about how the entire team does. The weakest link of the chain will never be allowed to falter, since everyone will pitch in the moment they sense trouble.

The players are extremely flexible and adaptable because they have no pre-set agenda or real purpose other than to work together with the other players successfully. What has been unspoken thus far is the absence of an ego, as an ego can completely sabotage and destroy what is being carefully created.

Improv players work together like cyclists, with the front cyclist taking his turn at the front of the line to absorb all of the wind resistance, then falling back and letting someone else pick up the slack. Of course, that would never work if someone's ego were to get in the way and they decided they were bigger than the team. The whole line would be disrupted and rendered useless.

If none of what I've described resembles how you've approached conversations or interactions up to this point in your life, it's time to re-evaluate your approach. Improv players spend years toiling away perfecting their craft, but we don't have to get to Will Ferrell's level to simply improve our conversations. We can greatly increase our conversational intelligence simply by imagining a collaborative and accepting process. You are in fact working towards a shared goal with someone, so it's time to start acting like it. There is a necessary give and take, and sacrificing the spotlight must occur in order to reach this shared goal. Even if the person you're talking to doesn't realize it, the burden must fall on you to make it happen. Flexibility and the ability to adapt are paramount to any great conversation.

Make It Easy (for Others to Be Lazy)

Improv players are focused on making the performance as a whole shine, and they know they do that by giving others easy setups and premises to work with. They're not going to give others a scenario they know nothing about with a complete lack of details.

In addition to giving each other as many "softballs" as possible, they'll support each other and be on board, no matter how dire it gets. Someone will swoop in to rescue you, and you can depend on their help. It builds a sense of security and space for vulnerability to try new things and otherwise open up. Everyone is each other's best supporting actor or actress. Now, that's a powerful feeling to have about someone you are speaking with.

There are many ways we can similarly make it easier for the person we converse with to speak their mind or express themself. Display openness. Solicit opinions and ask questions. Put others in the spotlight and allow them to shine. Don't put others in a conversational place to twist in the wind.

Improv comedy is one of the best things you can learn for your ability to think on your feet, excel at witty banter, and know what to say. That being said, it's also one of the scariest. It thrives on unpredictability, the very thing that most people hate. Many stray from social interaction and conversation because it can be so unpredictable. *What if it's awkward, they hate you, think you're weird, or don't laugh at any of your jokes?*

This compels some people to have a script in their head every time they talk to people in an attempt to make it less unpredictable and more comfortable. However, that of course takes you away from the present and the person in front of you. Once you become more familiar and comfortable with the principles of improv, you will see the heights you can reach as a result of creating unplanned *flow*.

React to Everything

One of the biggest challenges by neophyte conversationalists and improv players is reading people accurately. It's definitely a skill that requires practice.

I distinctly remember an instance of speaking to a fellow attorney at a networking event years ago. I had said multiple times that I needed to find the bathroom, and that I needed to go soon, but he just didn't take the hint. Every time I would say it, he would launch into another story about himself. I eventually realized he couldn't read people. Finally, I interrupted him mid-story and waltzed away gracefully.

It didn't take a mastermind to read me in that situation, but rarely is reading people's emotions and state of mind so clear and obvious. Players in improv comedy have to do the impossible on a daily basis—ascertain what someone is trying to communicate based on *very* few cues.

At first, you might not catch the cues. Once you learn what they are, you'll start to spot them more and more. As you get better, you'll be able to see them coming before they even emerge, because there are certain patterns that always arise.

For instance, an eye roll can mean many things in isolation, but when you pair an eye roll with restless body language and a scoff, it probably means that someone is bored with you.

Getting better at reading people is the first step to this chapter's rule of reacting properly. You wouldn't react to a story about a friend's death with laughter, so it's important that your read and your reaction are congruent with each other. Sometimes we instinctually just know, like when we laugh when a friend tells a bad joke, or when someone shows you a video and you know that you're supposed to laugh when they do.

How can you read people better? It starts with what they talk about, and how much they talk about it. In fact, for the purposes of this book, it's the most important part. Just listen to them.

People drop hints in conversation all the time. There's a reason they bring up what they bring up, and what they seem to want to dwell on.

There's a reason people speak in deeper, specific detail about some things, and will continually steer the conversation back even after they go on a tangent. It's important to them and they want to share it with you.

For example, if someone keeps talking about their dog, or seems to mention them in an offhand manner multiple times, this is a breadcrumb for you to follow. Rarely will people say, "I want to talk about my dog, listen to me now," as opposed to shoehorning it semi-organically into an existing conversation.

You're looking for these breadcrumbs that others want you to pick up on so they can talk about what they want.

Let me backtrack and reiterate. People will literally tell you what they're interested in by what they talk about. They'll either bring it up spontaneously and on their own, or speak about a subject with a measure of excitement and joy. Those are your indicators for how to read people, but they require you to really pay attention to the other person and above all else, stop speaking so you can hear them.

If they don't have energy or excitement about a topic, or they appear to switch topics spontaneously, then it's clear that they aren't interested in it. People won't outright say that they want to talk about certain topics, so it's up to you to pick up on their hints and react accordingly.

Of course, there is also the non-verbal portion of reading people. For the purposes of this book, we'll keep it simple. You have to know only one thing: the baseline of body language of the other person. In other words, what are someone's facial expressions and body language when they feel normal and are not expressing an emotion?

For example, some people might naturally be bubbly and speak with their hands, and others might be as still as a wooden doll even when they're ecstatic. This baseline can let you know when someone deviates from it, and then you can interpret their body language accordingly. If the aforementioned person who is incredibly still even when happy shows a hint of motion and emotion, you can safely assume that they are overjoyed, or upset, by something.

Again, these are the breadcrumbs that people want you to find, and this is especially true the better people get with conversation. Conversation at the highest levels becomes all shades of gray and subtlety because both parties pick up on the signals being exchanged. Much of what it is said during an exchange of witty banter is subtext and between the lines, so to speak, because both parties operate on multiple levels.

Here are some common breadcrumbs:

The excitement, or lack thereof, in someone's voice when you bring up a topic.

If someone keeps trying to bring up a topic, this means they want to talk about it.

If someone keeps looking away, this means that they are bored.

If someone's feet are pointed away from you, this means they want to stop talking to you.

If you interrupted someone right as they were about to
speak, ask them about it after you finish speaking to
see what direction they were interested in going.

See if you can tell if their smiles and laughs are fake or real,
depending on how big they are and how quickly they fade or
stop.

If someone ignores what you say and goes back to what
they were talking about before you spoke, they feel
strongly about their point and want to expand on it.

If someone leans their head on their hand, this means
they might be bored with the current flow of the
conversation.

Look for how strongly someone nods in agreement with you,
and on the flip side, how little excitement or emotion there is
in their reaction.

The final aspect of getting better at instantly reading people is to think in terms of emotions. Whatever someone says
or demonstrates to you through their body, they are doing it
to create an emotional response.

A story about their dog feeding a kitten? They want a
happy smile.

A story about being cut off in traffic? They want shared
agony.

A statement about their foot being run over by a bike?
They want a laugh.

These are all emotions that people want to evoke in you, so
give it to them! That's the final aspect in a nutshell: proactively

think about the underlying emotion people want to evoke in you, and then give it to them. It sounds like it would be incredibly difficult to do in the spur of the moment, but it's easier than you think since there are only so few emotions that want back from you.

Here are the essential emotions people are looking to evoke: joy, anger, humor, annoyance, amazement, and curiosity.

If you think about most of what people have told you in the past week, and what you have told others, that short list covers almost all the bases for the emotional responses that were sought. They cover the bulk of the reasons that we share stories about our lives.

A story about their dog feeding a kitten—what is the reason that someone is telling you about this? Is it so you can feel annoyance? Amazement? Joy? It's probably a mixture of humor and joy. Show them that you understand and give them the reaction that they expected.

In fact, exaggerate your reactions. Not by too much, just enough so that it's unmistakable the emotion that you're feeling.

There is a thin line between being emotionally touched by somebody's shared information, and mocking that person by caricaturing their emotions. If you go overboard, you may seem like you're mocking and patronizing them. They will feel judged and insulted.

Instead, jump on board with them and their emotion. If they come to you with a story about how they were slighted, first show the appropriate matching emotion in a way that will make them feel acknowledged and validated. That's what matters first in reacting. What you do next can be any mixture of asking questions or validating more, but the initial reaction makes the biggest impact.

People have different levels of emotional intensity, and the middle of the bell curve as far as emotional expression is concerned can be quite wide. This simply means that people perceive and experience emotions differently, so what you think is an indulgent and overboard reaction may not register at all for someone else. This is the case for most people. They think they are conveying a message, but in reality have only managed a frown or smile.

It therefore pays to be slightly dramatic and overboard with your emotional reaction, just to ensure that you aren't being too subtle for your own good. Some of us have far better poker faces than we realize, so exaggeration is sometimes necessary to get our message across. Plus, a big reaction makes people feel good, as if they have bestowed us with valuable information.

A conversation is a two-way street.

You can't just say what you want, wait while the other person is talking, and then say what you want again as if they merely interrupted you. It's not just a simple matter of waiting for your turn to speak.

Conversation is about mutual sharing that leads to mutual listening and learning, otherwise it's just two monologues being directed towards each other. Hopefully, if you can acknowledge the importance of what they're saying to them, then they will do the same to you because they'll feel heard, validated, respected, and important.

This is going to feel unnatural and uncomfortable for some, but if you want your conversations to go deeper and last longer, then you need to play this game. Reactions aren't natural to all of us, and we may not even care about most of the things that people say. The goal is to improve our conversations, and you can't improve if you don't investigate new things that are out of your comfort zone.

One final thing: react to *everything*. This includes others' stories, gestures, looking at a phone, taking their jacket off, stretching their arms, questions about the same topic, puzzled facial expressions, tilting their head, an eye roll, an uncomfortable smile, and so on.

There may not be a flashing emotion to demonstrate, but they still did these things for a reason, and if you react to everything, you will show yourself to be 100 percent present with the other person.

Here's a good exercise to practice your reactions:

Pretend that you are mute while watching a television show, and react non-verbally to express the emotions that you interpret from the characters. Exaggerate these non-verbal reactions. Be sure to pause occasionally.

Facial expressions, body language, gestures, and eye contact are all key. Make sure that your true message is getting across. This is practice for you to react to others, and see what the range of reactions can be to demonstrate that you've heard them. You may also discover that you have to exaggerate your reactions a bit to be understood, and that something that seemed so obvious to you actually was not.

When you actively seek to understand the emotional state of people you're interacting with, which can be as simple as whether or not they are enjoying a topic of conversation, you're given a template for where to go and how to get there.

It is the opposite of thinking in a self-centered manner, which is clearly beneficial because there are at least two parties to a conversation.

It boils down to this: if someone conveys that they are angry and we completely miss it, an awkward and uncomfortable situation arises. When this happens frequently enough, people will tend to avoid you. If you can accurately catch the emotions people are conveying, even though they may not be saying it explicitly, they will feel that you understand them better and be more drawn to you.

Create Motion

When you have motion in a conversation, it's not that you are injecting it with energy and high spirits. It's that you can't stay on the same topic forever, and the conversation needs to evolve in one way or another, or else interest will be lost.

Let's look at this in the improv comedy context. Suppose that the starting topic for an improv scene is a visit to the dentist, and it begins in the lobby. Does the scene stay in the lobby? Absolutely not. It moves in at least one of a few ways.

The scene might move locations into the office of the dentist itself.

The scene might introduce multiple different characters.

The scene might change its focus and move away from the dentist altogether.

The scene might change the initial purpose and disclose that the patient is visiting the dentist because he is an assassin and the dentist is his next hit. And so on.

Contrast any of those situations to a scene that stays exactly in the same lobby, with the same characters. It may not be the worst scene, but it won't be able to introduce any of the interesting settings or details that would arise from *creating motion,* and that's what it means when an improv scene must go somewhere. You can't talk about the same thing in the same setting forever. Introducing new threads is always going to be more beneficial to the scene.

To boil it down to one main sentiment, the people involved in either a conversation or an improv scene will have an easier time if they intentionally create motion and seek to introduce new elements.

In normal conversation, for example, you can't talk about the weather forever. You need to create motion away from it, or into it from a different angle. It seems obvious that motion, and an interaction, must go somewhere would be necessary and beneficial, but many people will fall prey to one major trap with it. In the quest for motion and additional elements and angles, there is the danger of planning ahead with fixed ideas and destinations in mind.

This is dangerous for a few reasons.

First, imagine the concept of an improv comedy performance with three participants, and all three already have fixed ideas of where they want to scene to go. In essence, they will be influencing each other with each trying to herd the other two into the directions that they want. It won't be teamwork; it'll just be teammates trying to exert control over each other in front of an audience. It won't be pretty unless you like hearing three monologues simultaneously.

Second, you run the risk of spectacular failure when you are derailed from the path of your fixed destination. This is because you are so fixated on the destination that you haven't kept an open mind to other subjects or topics, and won't be able to adapt very well.

If you've been thinking the whole time about how to turn the conversation or performance to the subjects of cars, you will probably come up tongue tied when the subject instead turns to different types of hats. If you are open to the destination, you can roll with the punches, so to speak, because your mental bandwidth isn't otherwise consumed.

Third, having a fixed destination in mind for your conversation or improv performance makes you too goal-oriented, and by definition this means you are willfully ignoring everything else that happens in front of you. You might even be dismissing them because they aren't what you are looking for.

Suppose that you want to arrive at the same topic of cars, and other topics keep getting in the way. Being overly goal-oriented would lead you to continually bring up cars, even though it would be a completely random shift in topic, and unwelcome since it was steered away from multiple times. It makes you appear tone deaf, and people will begin to wonder if you've even heard them speak. It also generally makes you a fairly un-engaging conversationalist.

Creating motion is preferred, but you can't necessarily plan ahead for it. That defeats the open-ended nature of improv comedy that makes it so engaging and entertaining.

Instead, you can plan for your conversations to resemble stories and movies, and learn about specific types of motion you can introduce on the fly.

When you go to a movie, you're not looking for something that fits your daily life. You're looking for a story about something significant, unusual, or extraordinary, a deviation from your daily life. If you're going to watch a biographical movie, you wouldn't want to watch the mundane parts where they use the bathroom and brush their teeth.

Instead, you want to see the unique, interesting, and exaggerated parts. You want to see conflict, problem solving, then resolution. These are all accomplished by creating motion in normal conversation topics, and not just staying in one place.

A conversation that stays in one place will eventually become boring filler, since topics can easily be exhausted without motion. As I mentioned before, there are only so many comments or questions you can make about the weather. So, how do you create motion in a topic such as the weather?

Types of motion:

- Change to a topic related to the weather.
- Go deeper into the topic of weather, beyond shallow and surface-level comments.
- Share a personal experience with weather.
- Ask what their favorite types of weather are.
- Talk about the emotions the weather invokes in you.
- Talk about your nuanced opinion on the weather.
- Ask outlandish hypothetical questions about the weather.
- Reference third parties (papers, articles, statements from friends) regarding the weather.

Note that these are similar ways of creating motion as the ways of manipulating the scene at the dentist's lobby from earlier in this chapter. They force the interaction to go somewhere, and don't allow it to remain on comments about the weather, or to stay in the dentist's lobby.

Another way to think about creating motion in conversation is that it's a measure of conversational agility. Before one topic is completely bled dry, you can jump to other ones to keep engagement high and prevent stagnation.

Stagnation is one of the sneakier causes of poor interactions because it's something that we all do eventually. It's the lazy person's way of conversing—relying on the other person to shoulder the burden of topics and details. This rule of creating motion battles stagnation, as it forces you to move away from lazy routines.

Let's take another example where the topic is suddenly steak.

Types of motion:

- What made you bring up steak and why it was on your mind?
- What memories do you have with steak?
- How has your view of steak changed over the years?
- A random fact or piece of trivia you know about steak.
- Your emotions regarding steak.
- Ask for others' emotions regarding steak.

Great stories and great conversations are journeys. They never remain in the same place. There is a sense of direction, there is a sense of conflict that needs resolution, and there is a sense of tension that needs to be unwound. It's not a preset place that you end up in, and there's a sense of closure. There's a payoff, and that's what creating motion does.

Conversation Threading

Conversation threading is another technique for practicing how to reply to people and actually think faster in the middle of conversation.

Like free association, it is also a matter of looking at what is right in front of you and using it.

Let's take a simple sentence you might be faced with in conversation that you have no idea how to respond to, for instance, "I went skiing with my brother last weekend."

You could reply with, "Oh, how interesting," or something similarly vague that doesn't move the conversation forward. Conversation threading begs you to look at what was said in a few steps.

Step one: break the statement down into specific elements.

I went skiing [element one] with my brother [element two] last weekend [element three].

Step two: comment on or ask a question about any of those elements.

If you view a statement as a single piece of rope, then each element is a potential thread that you could grab onto and use and focus on. In other words, once you know what a statement is compromised of, you can ask or comment specifically on any of those elements. You are probably getting more information to work with than you think.

In the above example, you could ask about skiing, you could ask about their brother and family, or you could ask for other details about that weekend or another weekend. Those are just some of the threads you can pick up after breaking down that simple statement.

Conversation threading seeks to break conversation down into bite-sized elements that you can use. We often get into our heads about what to say or think, and we then lose track of what's going on in front of us. We are trying to process conversation in our minds, but in doing so, aren't able to hear, "A, B, C, and D," and simply reply, "Oh, how was A?"

Here's another example statement to break down: "The sandwich at the corner café was a little stale. I would not recommend it."

The sandwich [element one] at the corner café [element two] was a little stale [element three]. I would not recommend it [element four]."

Off the top of my head, you can ask or comment about:

- The type of sandwich
- The café's ambiance
- Their favorite type of sandwich
- What "stale" means to them
- Whether they would recommend any other food or drink from the café
- Whether it was their first time there
- Where they would recommend for a good sandwich
- Whether they like burgers or sandwiches more

Breaking things down is like highlighting keywords in a textbook so you can make notes with them later.

When you start to look at people and break down what they say, you might notice a couple of things. First, that people aren't really trained to give many details in their answers, and they won't always be giving you so much to work with. Not every statement can be very fruitful. Instead of ABCD, you might only have AB, but that's still something to work with. Remember, people are lazy. This also means that instead of merely asking or commenting on A or B, you have to find different ways of engaging on a single topic—something we'll cover later.

Second, you're lazy as well. You are likely guilty of giving people terrible answers that they can't work with or ask about easily. If you've ever wondered why people might walk away from you sometimes, the answer just might be you—*you* might be why. You're not making it easy for others, breaking one of our cardinal rules.

So looking at yourself through the lens of conversation threading can be a kind of assessment tool for yourself and the people around you—who's making it easy for others and who is doing the bare minimum? Hopefully, you fall into the former group.

Conversation threading is initially something that might make you less socially fluent, especially in the middle of a flowing conversation, but it gets easier as it becomes a habit.

Interrupting Selectively

Most books and pieces of advice on conversation will advise that you never, ever interrupt others.

They'll invariably say that interrupting is rude and sends the wrong message to other people. It's selfish and violates the golden rule of conversation, which is to let others talk about themselves *ad nauseum.*

Okay . . . there's some truth to that.

If you interrupt constantly and don't let people get on track with what they want to say, they will eventually start to hate you because you will come off as selfish and self-absorbed. And honestly, you probably are if you find that you constantly interrupt. You also aren't building the connection you think you are because you are constantly focusing inwardly.

The ironclad rule about interrupting is fairly incorrect . . . but it's also easy to misuse the contents of this chapter, so interrupting artfully is a concept that you have to be careful with.

When you talk to someone, there are several levels of communication happening simultaneously. People can feel just fine consciously, yet have a negative feeling subconsciously . . . if they are continually interrupted in a way that rubs them the wrong direction.

Keep this in mind because there will be a point where you might end up stepping on somebody's toes.

So how do you interrupt artfully, and avoid the negative feelings that might be associated with interruptions?

Interrupting to Agree

Just as the above says, interrupt only to agree. Interrupt because you are in fact so excited about what they are saying, that you can't hold it in!

Similarly, interrupt to complete that person's sentence, and interrupt to show that you are emotionally present with them.

Allow me to illustrate.

> *I was just in Greece and loved it when . . .* [interruption]
> *No way! That is so exciting and Greece is my favorite place in the whole world!*

And then I tried parking there and the meter maid . . .
[interruption] *Was terrible and ticketed you anyway
despite the sign, right?! She's the worst.*
That movie was amazing, I just couldn't believe when . . .
[interruption] *The ending, right?! It was such a
shocking and crazy twist!*
I couldn't believe it, I absolutely . . . [interruption] *Hated
that book, right?! I totally agree!*

What do you notice about the examples above? They all
denote a level of excitement for what the other person is
talking about. The excitement is actually so high, and you feel
the same way that they do, that you can't wait for them to
finish!

So you are interrupting with a purpose, and not just
blindly to interject something randomly about yourself. You
are interrupting to agree, commiserate, show your emotional
engagement, and *feel* together.

You are also interrupting because you feel as strongly
about the subject as they do. You have the same level of emotional urgency, and that is key. Instead of challenging them,
you are firmly agreeing, and who doesn't like to be agreed
with?

The more they feel you are in the same emotional place as
them, the more they will like you.

But hey, we don't always feel so emotionally identical to
other people so as to finish their sentences. What if we just
want to create that feeling of closeness?

It's not difficult to actually predict what people are saying
so that you can interrupt to agree, or finish their sentences.

You can usually tell when they are getting worked up, and when people get worked up, they make big proclamations. They even use hyperbole.

So . . . isn't it easy to see where you can interrupt? If you know they feel strongly about something, interject there!

For example, you are talking about laptop computers. It becomes apparent that they enjoy Apple products a lot.

Gosh, I can't believe that person has a PC, it's so . . . [interruption] *I know, why can't they just come to the dark side with Apple? Such superior products!*

Of course, this can backfire on you if you guess the wrong way. For example, if in the above example you guessed that the other person loved PC products instead of Apple products.

There's an easy solution for this as well. You simply interrupt them but don't finish your sentence.

For example: *I know! It's so . . .*

And then you allow other person to finish the statement with *amazing!* or *horrible!* so you can see which direction they are going.

You Just Get Them

Let's face it: modern life can occasionally be alienating and isolating.

At some level, most people feel that few people truly get who they are. Whether or not this is true, it's a mindset that motivates us every day.

When you speak in unison with somebody, this creates emotional unison. You both get emotionally engaged and these "aha" moments can't help but draw you closer to each other.

These types of moments create the impression of a deep and profound understanding. If this happens frequently through your conversation, the person you're talking to can't help but feel hopeful. They can't help but get a feeling that the person they're talking to, which is you, truly gets them.

If you're trying to become a really great conversationalist and you want to be persuasive, this is a powerful element that can work to your favor. These are all things that precede bonding inside jokes from shared experiences, which leads to the impression of "you and me against the world."

"We . . ." As annoying twins often say, they are so close that they can finish each other's sentences. What they might not realize is that it works the opposite way as well—if you can finish each other's sentences, you can create the feeling of familiarity and closeness.

The Four-Word Magic Phrase

This one phrase is how I became one of my supervisor's favorite employees at one of my first jobs in a small shoe store.

At the time, I was young so I didn't really have any idea how to act in a more professional setting. It was tough to feel comfortable, and most of the time I had no idea what to say. So when I talked to my supervisor, I would ask questions about the store and how much stock was coming in the next day.

He seemed overly enthusiastic whenever I used the phrase, "What were you saying?" which I only used because I had no idea what to say, and this tactic has grown from there.

You should look into using this phrase often. It actually applies to a lot more situations than you might imagine. If you aren't using it at all, it may mean that people are probably not enjoying speaking to you as much as you would like to believe. You might be thinking you are a great conversationalist, but if you're not using this phrase, chances are quite high that others don't think so.

This magical phrase does more than redirect topics; it lets people know you're listening and actively care about what they're saying.

It can be used in just about any situation where topics start overlapping, or people get too excited to focus on one thing at a time, but here are some specific conversational hotspots in which to use "What were you saying?"

When You Interrupt Someone and They Let You Keep Speaking

This is when you barge into someone's statement and they actually let you keep speaking and interrupt them completely.

After you're done with your piece, use this phrase to tell the other person that what they had to say is important, and you are asking them to continue despite your outburst. It also lets the other person remember that they were saying something before, and that they aren't obliged to continue on your line of conversation.

Try, as much as possible, not to interrupt others. But when you do, saying "What were you saying?" can be a life-saver for the conversation.

When You Begin Speaking at the Same Time as Someone

During conversation, it often happens that you begin speaking simultaneously with someone else.

What happens in those cases? One person has to gracefully bow out and allow the other to continue. Always try to be that person by saying, "Sorry, what were you saying?"

It gives way to them, and it lets them feel that you respect them. You yield the floor. And of course, it's not like your topic or thought is lost forever. It's just next in line, which is not bad for a conversation involving just two people.

When You Go Off on an Extended Statement, Story, or Rant

You are speaking at the right time and it's your turn. The problem is you've gone on for too long. It was long-winded, drawn out, and probably boring for the other person. This applies not only to a statement, but also to a story or rant. If you can catch yourself going on too long, slip in the phrase, "What were you saying?" to shift the gravity back to the other speaker and show self-awareness of your extended statement.

When You Want to Make the Other Person Feel More Involved in the Conversation

If you're talking to more than one person, it's almost a certainty that at least one of those people will feel left out. This is completely natural because when you are engaged in a conversation, one person might be engaged while the other person feels left out.

Don't feel too bad. Just reel the other party back in by saying this phrase. You don't want them to feel left out. This simple phrase reminds them that they're part of the conversation. Try to make sure the flow of the conversation is evenly distributed among the participants and one is struggling to conceal a yawn.

Simply, this tells the other person that you're not full of yourself. We often unintentionally make people feel powerless. This often takes place when one person takes over the conversation. While most people are more than happy to listen, eventually they reach a point where they feel they really don't have any skin in the game as far as the conversation goes. They're just the spectator, and the other person is the performer.

No matter how interesting you may think you are, always remember that conversations are two-way streets.

Using this statement reverses any feeling of powerlessness or disenfranchisement. You may have monopolized the conversation, but this statement can heal whatever bruised emotions or damaged egos may be involved. If nothing else, people will feel less like hostages to the conversation.

Variations of This Phrase

There are many different ways you can say this phrase, and they all pretty much work the same way. However, some phrases make better sense in certain contexts. I'll leave it up to you to figure out how to tweak the following phrases to maximize their effect. Still, it's very important to keep in mind your overall goal of drawing people back into the conversational spotlight.

- "Back to you."
- "Sorry for interrupting, please go on."
- "Was that what you were going to say?"
- "I'll shut up now. What do *you* think?"

Think of it as a verbal boomerang. For some reason or other, the conversation went off track and at some point it became uncomfortable. Conversation is about building a mutual level of comfort and confidence. Restore the conversational balance and you're on the right path.

Throw the Ball Back

Awkward silences are one of conversation's biggest enemies, and they seem to be everywhere. Of course, the more you think about them, the more you seem to be unable to escape them.

But awkward silences almost always follow a repeatable pattern that you can stop immediately.

Imagine a conversation is like a game of catch. The ball goes back and forth just like the dialogue and who takes their turn to speak. But then, imagine that your partner drops the ball and you are left waiting without anything to do.

That's exactly what an awkward silence is. Instead of the conversation flowing from person to person, someone has dropped the ball and not thrown it back, though they think they have. A silence then follows because both people believe that they are waiting for the ball to be thrown to them, when in reality, one of them actually has the ball and is just not using it properly.

In other words, awkward silences occur because it's someone's turn to speak but they don't realize it. Thus, they are waiting for the other person, and nothing happens because no one wants to feel like they are interrupting the other.

It sounds like it would be obvious to know when you've thrown the ball back, but most of the time, it's not so direct.

Most of the time when we don't throw the ball back, it's because we are just acknowledging someone instead of adding to the conversation, sharing something, or asking a question.

An acknowledgment by itself adds nothing and is just a verbal nod of the head. The other person might assume you are going to follow it up with something, but the acknowledgment just lets them know you heard them.

> Jill: "And then I just told him to get out of my apartment!"
>
> Bob: "Ah, interesting."

Bob isn't going to say anything else because he thinks he has done his part in throwing the ball back by acknowledging the statement. Jill isn't going to say anything because she thinks Bob might have more to say, and Bob hasn't added anything for her to reply to.

And that's how awkward silences are born the vast majority of the time—innocently forgetting that you have the ball and neglecting to throw it back to the other person. Throw the ball back to prevent awkward silences!

The easiest way to always make sure you are throwing the ball back, if you are the one at fault, is to more frequently *lead the interaction*.

Leading the interaction means what it sounds like—it's when you take responsibility for the conversation and take on the burden of making sure it flows. If there's any lull or silence, you take it upon yourself to fill it. If you are too in the weeds on a topic or you find yourself talking about the weather for ten minutes, you take it upon yourself to change topics to something mutually enjoyable.

Imagine this: You were setting out on a long two-month trip through Europe. Sounds like a grand old time. Suppose you were going with a friend, but you knew your friend was hopeless with a map and planning. Pretty much the worst travel partner ever, but you enjoy their company so much it's not an issue.

What role would you then take? You would fill in the gaps and take ownership over everything because you know you'd have to, otherwise nothing would get done.

That's the exact approach you should have when you are leading the interaction. Assume they will do nothing and you will have to do all the heavy lifting. It's shocking how much that can change your approach to things, such as preventing awkward silences. You would certainly never fail to throw the ball back to someone, and even compensate when someone doesn't throw the ball back to you.